THE STAGES OF A MAN'S LIFE

The Stages Of A Man's Life

A Guide for Men and Women

E. James Wilder

Quiet Waters Publications
Bolivar, Missouri
2003

Quiet Waters Publications
P.O. Box 34, Bolivar, MO 65613
E-mail: QWP@usa.net
For other titles, prices, and order information:
www.quietwaterspub.com

Cover design by Myron Sahlberg.

Second, revised edition 2003.

ISBN 1-931475-18-0

CONTENTS

PREFACE

In a time of gender identity confusion, E. James Wilder's book feels like a cleansing rain bringing down eye-stinging clouds of dust that blocked the view. It is refreshing to read how Dr. Wilder breaks the typical mold of pop-psychology by resisting the temptation to offer a number of behavior-modifying steps. Instead, his experienced insight reveals an inside view of what is visible only from the outside.

As an answer to legitimate questioning and attempts to re-define the male in our society, Dr Wilder's "stages" evolve around a crucial principle: any ability to give is based on the grace to receive. Somehow we were brought up believing it is more masculine to take rather than to receive. Receiving seems to be associated with weakness - and no man wants to be weak.

According to Dr. Wilder, receiving is the more difficult and neglected part in our growth towards masculine maturity. The adult man, the father, the elder is not so much characterized by self- sufficiency and independence as by loving responsibility and interdependence.

Responsibility, the ability to respond to values, is the key. We need to receive from mother, father, other men, elders, and community to become aware of who we are and who we were meant to be. Unaware of our own beauty, we may walk through a spring meadow without seeing or enjoying a single flower. Where this value is experienced, needs can be expressed. To have no needs is inhuman, not manly. The more a boy and later the man is able to express those needs and thankfully receive what he needs, the more sensitive he will become to others unique needs. Instead of reducing his tension passively through immediate and indiscriminate gratification, the redeemed man actively pursues value-oriented achievements.

Once we have grasped the principle, there are many gems to be discovered in this clear and concise book. The author's liberating authenticity lets us share in "his-story" of receiving with every page. Above all, Dr. Wilder rekindles the joy, the adventure, the romance, and the promise of fulfillment of being a man. May all, including myself, who are on their way and who feel the calling to become men, fathers and elders be blessed by the insights of this book and take them to heart.

Dr. Daniel Trobisch
Psychotherapist, Salzburg, Austria

INTRODUCTION

Many men still feel like little boys inside. Many of us have trouble pinpointing when we became men. We are not quite sure what it means to be a man. We are born babies, grow into boys, then men, often becoming fathers, and finally elders.

For each phase of life, there are tasks to be mastered. When you paint a house you begin with a primer and then add the finishing coats, one step at a time. Growing up male is a five-step process. If we get the steps in the right order and do a reasonably good job on them, we will be satisfied with the results. Otherwise, like a bad paint job on a house, we will be cracking, blistering, and peeling every time things get hot.

Why is it that men aren't more in touch with themselves? Many men actually hate themselves. We read in the story of creation (Gen 1:31): God looked at everything that he had made, "and behold, it was good!"

To reach maturity every man must go through several life stages and complete the essential tasks. Each stage builds on the previous one. We either go through them or wish that we had. Here are the stages:

The Unborn— Grows a body

The Infant— The baby grows a joyful individual identity and learns his needs and feelings

The Boy— Learns to take care of himself

The Man— not only knows his own needs and feelings, but is able to satisfy the needs and feelings of others

The Father— Gives life to others

The Elder—   reaches beyond his own household to help
others

If you work diligently at each of these steps and keep them
in the right order, you will be blessed and admired as a mature, fulfilled, and fruitful man. You will remind everyone that
being a man, just as being a woman, is really a good thing.

E. James Wilder

I. AN INFANT

1. GROWING UP

Birth

"It's a boy!" What a good thing has happened—a boy has been born and that is just what God planned. After such a good start will he become the man that God intended him to be?

The Six Stages of Man

Six stages describe the growth of each man or woman. Each has its own demands and builds upon the earlier stages. Perhaps it will take one's whole life to understand the importance that the first stages have for the last ones. What seems complex at first becomes a single, deep and complex rhythm of variations of the same theme—how to receive and then to give life.

Unborn—	the unborn life grows a body
Infant—	the baby develops a joyful individual identity through receiving
Child—	the boy learns to take care of himself
Adult—	the man develops his "group identity" and takes care of two or more people at the same time
Parent—	the father gives life without needing to receive in return.
Elder –	the elder directs the growth of his community's identity.

We will say little in this book about the unborn stage of growth. What we must notice, however, is that growing up is not automatic. Physical growth does not mean that maturity will follow. Regrettably, many men are still infants or children developmentally when they should be fathers or elders.

It is also unwise to rush development ahead of time. The stages in this book are the ideal. They cannot be achieved ahead of time, but they can take much longer when a man does not complete his work or if his family and community fail to provide the help he requires at each stage. Each stage achieved at the optimal time will look like this:

Infant—   birth through three
Boy—   four through twelve
Man—   thirteen through birth of first child
Father—   first child until youngest child becomes adult
Elder—   youngest child reaches thirteen until death

I have chosen these stages because they match common words used in many cultures and languages. More importantly, these are also the terms used in scripture when describing the different stages of maturity. There are cultural, scriptural, and physical reasons to choose the ages for each stage.

While containing much value, growing up does nothing to increase our value as human beings. Infants are as valuable as fathers—as the parents of every newborn baby know. Many men are ashamed of their immaturity and feel they will lose their value if they admit they are still infants and children inside. With the courage to admit where we are in our development comes the first solid starting point in life. This book is a guide for those growing up on schedule and for those who are catching up.

Becoming an Infant

It may sound strange to speak of becoming an infant, but like all stages of growth, we are not very accomplished when we

THE STAGES OF A MAN'S LIFE / 15

first begin. The infant's task is to learn to receive what he needs and express what he feels in a way that fits him. Little boys are not born knowing what they want or feel—it must be learned.

Boys and men need to know that the foundation of life is to be able to receive what we have not earned without shame. The need to receive is with us all of our lives. We will need this skill in every later stage—as children, men, fathers, and elders. We express our needs and receive without condemnation or shame.

Just as each stage of life has its job, each job has its purpose. The purpose of the first stage of development is to learn about grace. This is how we learn about our intrinsic value. The twelve years of boyhood are the time to learn how to receive grace. Grace is a gift given freely, not dependent on performance.

All of us have value, because we are created in God's image. We have value because God has said that we do. It is not because of anything we have done.

A moment of self-examination will cause many people to discover that they feel their value comes from what they can do. If they couldn't earn a living they would question their value. Boys who never learn how to receive grace become men who turn to achievements, fame, and fortune in order to find value.

Our culture is not going to tell us who we really are. God tells us we have great value for just being made in his image, so it is only if we look at ourselves from His point of view that we realize we are valuable, even if we can't do anything.

The need to receive is with us all of our lives. We will need this skill in every later stage of our lives—the stage of becoming a man, of becoming a father and of becoming an elder.

There is no way to talk about a boy and his needs or feelings without discussing his relationship to the two most important figures in his life, his mother, and father. The next two chapters will discuss a boy and his mother and a boy and his father, whether the boy's parents were physically present to him or not.

2. A BOY AND HIS MOTHER

But Mary treasured all these things and pondered them in her heart.
Luke 2:19

Our second son was born at home on the kitchen table. Before the cord was cut, he had cried and started nursing at his mother's breast. His mother had wanted him to be born at home surrounded by family.

Within the first two minutes of birth, he cried to express his need and then received from his mother's supply of milk. Our baby was learning to receive touch, food, comfort, and other things he never knew that he needed.

Mother and the Infant Son

To understand what it takes to be a baby boy, we need to look intimately at the infant's needs. Meeting these needs is his first order of business for the next four years. A boy needs a breast or a baby bottle. It will keep him alive, comforted and connected to his world. The breast then becomes a metaphor for the life-giving bond between son and mother. Although the sensual, emotional, and nutritional value of breast-feeding cannot be matched, it is the nature of the bond between son and mother that is of crucial concern, not whether the boy gets his nutrients and calories from his mother's breast or a baby bottle. For the next four years, she will be largely responsible for the quality of his life until he is weaned and ready to care for himself.

Take a few moments to imagine a baby boy's world. The baby's new world is a very unfamiliar place of sudden changes and few constants. In the midst of confusion there are the regular and relaxing workouts at Mother's breast. This connection brings life. From this experience, he begins to understand all other connections in his life. This is how basic trust begins to grow, for without this core the boy will mistrust the world and himself.

The boy asks and receives. He learns that he needs something and he learns to ask.

It is with Mother's help that the boy will learn that he has needs. Mother recognizes and intuitively knows that his cries ask for something. From within her come the words to fulfill his request. In time the boy learns to use words to express his needs until words are expected from him.

It is not my intention to tell mothers how to be mothers. I am explaining to men what a mother is like in relation to her baby boy so that men can understand.

Mother is the first source of connection for a boy. With Mother's help, the boy learns how to find all the essential things he will ever really need. He also learns about his own body—where it starts and ends, its powers and limitations.

The mother of a dependent infant is truly a marvel of creation. This mother knows his physical needs as well as when he needs attention or is curious. Furthermore, she thinks he is marvelous and lets him know that. This mother even likes to share her joy with others. She knows that he needs more love than her own and fills his life with good people before he knows he needs them.

Perhaps the main person that Mother shares him with is his dad, but older siblings are very important as well. The good mother finds other mothers for her child, so that he may benefit from more care and attention than she can provide. Love is not threatened by such sharing. Often these other mothers are female relatives. Sometimes they are close friends. Together they explore and enjoy the uniqueness of her son. He, in turn, learns that love is to be shared, not hoarded.

Pity the poor boy whose mother does not sense his needs or respond well to them. She meets his needs only when it is convenient. He approaches weaning with a desperate need to be connected because he hasn't yet forged a strong bond with his mother. Unlike other four-year-old boys who are eager to explore their father's world, take care of themselves, and make friends, he is concerned about being forgotten or left out. He senses that closeness to others will meet his need, but his bond with mother is not strong enough to bring satisfaction or security. For him, weaning will feel like further abandonment and rejection. As he grows up he will continue a desperate search for connection. He will fear being abandoned and rejected by women. He will fear his own needs. This is the man who will do anything for the love of a woman, yet never find her love to be enough. Rather than become an autonomous person, he develops shame and doubt about many things.

It is this early lack of connection with his mother that produces frantic men. Without this crucial time a boy will begin a sporadic, frantic search for connection with someone or something. Someone needs to be interested in who he is. Someone *has* to be interested in defining who he is. That special someone must find him interesting and approve of him.

An actor candidly told me, "I just can't resist it when a woman is attracted to me. I have to have that love. I can't turn it down." He has looked frantically through life for a connection that would tell him he is good, valuable, and interesting.

Tragically, many men have sexualized their need for connectedness, especially men who are attracted to pornography. They are looking for someone who is eager to be with them. Sex will not heal that wound; it cannot replace a mother or the Creator who is delighted to know you just the way you are.

The prophet Isaiah once wrote, "Can a mother forget the baby at her breast and have no compassion on the child she has borne? Though she may forget, I will not forget you!" (Isa 49:15). To get stuck in this early stage and replace the interest of a God who loves us like a mother nursing her child with unconnected sexual passion does not satisfy.

The boy who hasn't forged a bond with his mother senses this desperate need to be connected and lets it be known by seeking attention. If he has not been taught how he can meet his needs by asking, then he hopes that by getting attention from someone he will find what he needs. He has not learned to ask for what he needs. He is not ready to move from infancy to childhood.

Not all the bonds between mother and child are good. In fact, bonds can be generally sorted into two types: fear and love. Both can bond us to others and motivate our behavior. Fear and love can produce similar behavior, but in the case of a mother-and-son bond, fear produces defective connections.

Love allows us to see the other person for who he or she is. Contrary to the popular expression, love is not blind. To be a good mother to an infant, a mother must accurately sense the child's feelings and needs, and put words and actions to them. Her child will then feel understood and cared for. When the bond between mother and child is based on fear, then the mother can no longer see the boy and his needs clearly. She wraps him up in a blanket and feigns care in other ways because she is afraid of what other mothers will think of her. She keeps him from exploring because she is afraid he will hurt himself. She feeds him because she is afraid he will get sick or grouchy. She hushes his crying because she fears other will think she is a bad mother. As a result the boy does not learn his needs and does not trust his feelings. He learns his mother's fears instead. For such a boy, life becomes a long-term effort to keep people from becoming upset or afraid.

When bonds are based on fear, there is no way that any stage of growth can go right. The boy raised in fear will not know his own needs and feelings clearly. If a mother's fears are fairly realistic, then he will cope well with life; if her fears are exotic and irrational, he will have little chance of discovering who he really is.

When an infant has a close bond with his mother, she will appear and help him when something bad happens. From this he learns that he is not alone. The security of his bond with his mother serves as an anchor.

The stronger the bond with his mother, the greater will be his capacity to bond with the world around him. More importantly, he will neither fear those he loves nor try to control them.

Well-anchored children are usually invited by others to play with them. They allow other children to join in their play. Poorly anchored children beg to join other children. They are often rejected and end up playing alone. When they do succeed in playing with others, they frequently reject any additional playmates who want to join.

A true bond of love is characterized by joy, appreciation, encouragement, and the ability to risk. By contrast, the bond of fear is built on control, shame, or clinging. As with most of life, nothing is perfect. There are few perfect bonds of love or fear. Since love is stronger than fear, it sinks deeper into the soul. Still, a weak love will produce a bond that is easily overcome by strong fear. Strong love will withstand great fear.

Karin loved her children. She met their physical needs and played with them. As she shared them with her adoring husband, she appeared to be all a mommy could be for her infant son. But Karin had a deep fear of rejection, which she disregarded. True, she loved her husband and children and they loved her. But occasionally Karin would lose her temper with her son Justin. She was always very sorry afterwards, but she expected him to obey her at all times. Sometimes he ignored her. Justin's unresponsiveness awakened in Karin a fear she always carried that her own father's unresponsiveness meant he did not love her. This fear led her to try and scare a response out of Justin. This reliance on fear to connect with her son was a bond of fear with her father repeated with her son. Karin believes it is fear that connects parents with their children.

One function of a good mother is to notice her son's growth. She does not only attend to his physical needs. As she watches her son grow and change, she appreciates his uniqueness. Her appreciation will enable him to acknowledge his autonomy.

As each day passes the boy learns to ask and receive. His questions herald a transition to a world where he can start to stand on his own. He learns who he is.

Mother and Her Boy

With the help of his mother, an infant son learns to ask to have his needs met. He reaches the end of infancy and his dependence on Mommy to guess what he needs. The boy can now stand alone. This weaning involves a whole set of behaviors and attitudes whereby a boy begins to separate from the mother and achieve a basic level of independence. Mother is no longer in charge of guessing what the weaned boy needs and he must now ask for himself. He has learned to put words to his needs and feeling so that others can know him without having to read his mind.

No longer an infant or a baby, he is now a boy—a child. He begins taking care of one person, himself. It is not easy to build confidence, but through encouragement by his mother the child becomes successful at his new stage of independence.

After he has a successful start, his mother will steadily demand more from the boy. He will learn to ask correctly, at the right time, to the right person.

If a mother is not ready to let her son grow past infancy, then there may be endless fights about minor issues. If the mother relates to her son through her own fears, she will have trouble allowing him to learn from his own mistakes. Sometimes a mother tries to keep her son an infant by continuing to be his voice, by telling the world how to understand her son. It is not uncommon for such a mother to protect her son by covering for all his mistakes.

When his mother continues to be a stable source of warmth and care, the boy is free to try more difficult tasks, knowing that he has an anchor of comfort and acceptance. A mother's special gift is to help him know that he has value because he is her son, not because of his accomplishments.

Not everyone makes the transition from infant to child successfully. Some men spend the rest of their unhappy lives looking for someone who will know their needs without being told. They feel unloved if others do not guess what they want without verbal cues. "If I have to tell them or ask for something, it doesn't count," they say. These sad people never made it through weaning and still want love the way an infant child does.

In some ways we could describe the dysfunctional family as one in which a member who is old enough to feed himself expects his family members to feed him by guessing what he wants without asking. A little grunt, a turn of the head, or a tug at his coffee cup means he wants more coffee; and "Mother," whoever she is, must jump to meet "baby's" needs. How very much those actions resemble the infant's cries, turning his head towards his mother's breast or tugging on her blouse for his supper. If his needs are not met, he believes he has a grievance.

Men who are forced to become boys without first learning how to meet their infant needs will often react to breasts as though they were some extraordinary good thing regardless of whether the boy was breast fed or bottle fed. Not uncommonly such men have a fascination with breasts, particularly large ones.

The breasts are extraordinary if we consider the wonder of how a woman's body becomes a fountain of life, flowing with enough milk to sustain life and promote tremendous growth. But for the man stuck in infancy, breasts are a good object beyond his reach—a treasure cruelly kept from him by the powerful creatures that have them. Breasts are objects to be desired in a ceaseless fantasy to possess them.

Access to breasts can be an obsession with some men. There is no shortage of lingerie and clothing manufacturers willing to exploit the man who does not know what he really needs.

Girls who do not make the transition through weaning with the proper preparation to meet their own needs develop their own fascination with breasts. Girls wonder about the sufficiency of their own as measured by attractiveness and the current fashions. For the woman stuck in infancy, displaying and simultaneously hiding her breasts becomes an obsession. She seeks the perfect buxom figure to the point of enduring cosmetic surgery if clothing and padding do not suffice.

If a man and woman with infant level maturity meet, the resulting interaction gets physical rather quickly. Even if no touching occurs, the woman displays her attractions and the man works to possess her in some way and the woman tries to keep the man's attentions while keeping her distance. In this way she acts out her own interpretation of her mother's distancing after weaning.

The boy who has not completed his infant stage tasks does not know how to meet his needs by asking. He will quickly become angry. His frustration escalates as his anger triggers increasing rejection from others.

Mother and the Man

My wife Kitty went down to pick up our older son Jamie from college. It was the end of exam week. As they settled in for the two-hour drive home, my son said, "It's good to have you to myself all the way home. There are some things I want to talk to you about." Kitty was delighted. They went on to talk about girls, dating, surpassing one's own parents, and many other things.

Young men need to know whether they should fear the new power they have discovered within themselves. They instinctively turn to their mothers to see if they are securely anchored. Does Mom still find them lovable, or is she afraid of their newfound maturity? She is also a valuable keeper of her son's history. It is through his mother that he can learn what he was like before he was able to observe himself. He finds consolation and hope in the fact that his mother found him interesting, lovable and special even before he achieved his present accomplishments.

Mother's encouragement means so much at these times. Her faith in him brings the hope that he can be interested in new and unfamiliar worlds. The man who lacks this ability will find himself alone no matter how many friends or sexual experiences he has.

Mother for Her Grown Son, the Father or Elder

Mother-and-son relationships continue to be important throughout the son's lifetime. We read that the apostle Paul had been adopted by Rufus' mother who was very precious to him. We are never too old to appreciate someone with the ability to love us as ourselves.

One of the things that impressed me the most as a child about my dad was his relationship to his mother. As a busy missionary for over twenty-five years, my dad wrote to his mother every week. Every week she would write back. Almost all of her letters ended with, "Well, I see the mailman coming now, so I'd better get this in the mailbox." These words brought a picture to my dad's mind of his mother sitting by the window of the little house he had helped build on 422 Bauman Road with lilacs in front. He now lived in the countryside of Colombia, amidst constant threats to his life.

His mother reminded him of how God saw him, lovable and worth protecting.

A mother is at her best when she can see her son for who he is in God's sight; Mary kept all the things she heard about Jesus in her heart. A mother keeps the things about her children deep in her heart and she treasures them.

But What if Your Mother Is Dead?

There are two ways a mother can die. The most obvious death is physical. Once a man's mother has died physically it is important for him to remember her words and actions.

However, there is another form of death which is more insidious than the physical, when mother and son relationships exist only as a façade. A man comes to realize that his mother cannot see who he is in God's eyes. He is badly in need of adoption by a godly mother. Such adoptive mothers often have the gift of more vision about who we are. Like the apostle Paul, who treasured his adoptive mother, we should not be afraid of adoption.

II. A Boy

3. A Boy and His Father

The child grew and was weaned, and on the day Isaac was weaned Abraham held a great feast.

Genesis 21:8

Forming the Bond with Father

When my first son was born, I was elated to be a witness to something as marvelous as the ushering in of a new life. Anticipation was intense as I waited to meet and appreciate the child I had fathered.

As I called all the relatives to tell them the news, the question was asked time after time, "How are the mother and baby?" I began to wonder where the father fit in.

A father is important. He will engage in a myriad of physical activities with his son. As they play and develop these activities, the father and his son produce a bond that continues to enrich them both. A boy can be himself with his father and be appreciated for those things that make the boy unique.

Experiencing the Bond with Father

The baby boy who discovers his dad discovers a wonderful thing. His father appears and disappears in an almost random way. Dad represents the unpredictable, the exciting, the one who brings change. Being up on Daddy's shoulders is like riding an elephant or driving a fast car. It is awesome how much power the boy can control and direct.

Just as the infant boy needs a breast to receive life, so the baby boy needs a body of his own to experience that life. Dad, who has a body most like his own, is there to help the boy learn to live in his body. It is Dad who is best equipped to show the boy what he can do. To discover the boy's body and mind, they will play and work together. Together they will explore and expand the limits of his world. With Dad the boy will come into full possession of his body and mind. Together they will play. They don't have to test the limits, they just want to. Dad is very interested in the boy's abilities and wants him to try them out. Together they see what the boy can do.

The boy's bond with his father teaches him self-expression through play and work and how he influences his environment around him. He learns from the father that he can do things and make things happen. Fatherly influence offers him a rich variety of expressions.

Around Dad things are always going wrong. The boy learns that Dad smiles when he tries and misses. Together they can learn to laugh at mistakes and to test the limits.

Just as the mother cleared the way for the boy to know what he needed and felt because she was not afraid of his feelings or demands, the father helps the boy to grow past his fears of his limitations. A father's reassuring closeness helps him develop confidence.

So it is that the boy learns what he can and cannot do. He learns to receive and to create. His connections with his parents let him know he is valuable.

As the boy leaves infancy behind, Dad becomes a larger part of his life. Not only has Mother been teaching him how to ask for what he needs, but he has also been able to practice on Dad. Many times the results are remarkable. What a wonderful world for the boy! He knows that this enormous person is what he will be like when he is big. Just following the future around is fascinating.

Boys practice their identity as they go along. Much of this practice is what we call play. In play, boys try out their ideas of how to participate in life. Boys need to play. Play is the major way to learn identity during infancy and childhood.

Just as each phase of development builds on the previous one without removing it, there are ways in which development can be anticipated. Play often includes elements of preparation for future tasks. Kittens play in mock fights preparing for territorial disputes later on in life. They practice pouncing and stalking each other in preparation for hunting. Kittens lick each other in preparation for becoming mothers. In much the same way little boys also prepare to become men in their play.

You cannot spend much time around little boys without discovering that "fairness" is also important. While some writers think it is a bad thing that boys typically spend just as much time arguing about the rules as playing the game, rule setting is essential to play. Arguing is experimenting with the man's role of making things fair for all sides.

One way we helped our two sons Jamie and Rami (Rami rhymes with Jamie) prepare for fairness was to make it a family rule that they must work out conflicts between themselves. We gave them simple ground rules. If they brought a dispute to our attention or requested intervention they sat at a table where they remained until they both gave the other permission to leave. Sometimes negotiations were very loud and other times silent. Through this method they learned to realize the value of mutually acceptable solutions. Occasionally they were not able to solve the problems without adult help, and both agreed to find that help together. Adult intervention is key at times when real fairness is needed.

Sometimes brothers are asked to go beyond fairness and care for their brothers and sisters because the need is there. In this way a brother can also prepare a boy to be a father.

Provided that the practice is not too intensive and draining, most boys will find it gratifying.

Boys learn much from their mothers and fathers, but they practice what they learn with their siblings and peers. As you would expect, they compare lessons with each other as well as practicing. The influence of these practice sessions is considerable on every child's development. Parents who supervise these practice sessions well will find that they produce a strengthening of the lessons they have taught. But unexamined or unregulated play can often teach very different lessons to the boy about who he is or what he can do. The good father is attentive to this possibility and reviews his lessons frequently with his son.

Each member of the family exerts his or her influence. Individual uniqueness prevents us from making generalizations about each family member's role, but some generalizations about fathers will help us divide the work of parenting according to who is better equipped for a given task. This difference between a mother and a father is in some ways a difference in emphasis.

Fathers help their children focus and pursue their goals. However, under time pressure men usually lose their intuition and sensitivity if they are doing more than one activity at once. A father is not necessarily less intuitive than a mother. It is not that he lacks the capacity to sense what a child is feeling. If he has the time with his child he can provide these functions quite well. But the most intuitive man will usually become oblivious to others if he is trying to sort the mail, cook a meal, or plan his day. Women, on the other hand, are able to perform multiple tasks and maintain their sensitivity.

Fathers secure additional male role models for his sons. In doing so, the good father helps his son move towards the community of men and become someone greater than himself. By taking in the diversity of different men's fathering abilities, a boy will grow past his father's limitations and blind spots.

The Weaning Bond

Dad is also very important in helping a boy meet his needs. Helping his son take care of himself becomes the focus of his father's training once the day of weaning arrives. Weaning is the first major achievement that mother, father and child reach as a family team, and what an achievement it is.

Weaning is the second great transition in a child's life. In more traditional cultures, it is a specific time when breast-feeding stops, but its significance is the boy's readiness to feed and care for himself. It begins when a boy begins to meet his physical needs by himself. Unfortunately, we tend to rush weaning, rather than treasuring it by celebrating it as a milestone. It is a part of our son's history.

When Isaac was weaned Abraham held a feast. The day of his son's weaning the community was invited to share in the celebration as he was introduced to his community. The feast was a concrete way of showing that this boy was important, under his father's care and protection, and in need of the community's involvement. The feast let everyone know that while the boy had depended on his mother up to that point, his father was now responsible for him. His mother had brought him into the world through her labor. The father now brought him into the world surrounded by the fruits of his labor.

Isaac had learned what he needed and how to ask for it. He was now able to feed himself. A boy who could feed himself was ready for bigger adventures, and everyone rejoiced. He also learned that he did not feed himself in isolation.

Weaning is Dad's day in much the same way that the birth-day is Mother's day. Neither day would come to be without the other's efforts, but special changes take place in a boy's life that day that involve each parent in unique ways. Comforted by his father's voice and surrounded by his father's ample supply, the boy who can feed himself is now ready to learn many new aspects of his identity.

At weaning the father's role begins in earnest as he take the boy into the wider world. Each trip goes further from Mother's storehouse of supplies, but with Dad's help the boy discovers new sources.

Each adventure with Dad starts with leaving home and ends with a return to rest. And in this way the boy learns that both leaving and returning are good. Connecting and disconnecting in endless succession with no more fear than he felt releasing his hold on his mother's breast, the boy sets out to learn who he really is. Soon he will launch on his own adventures in the care of a watchful community which has been prepared by his father to receive him.

This process is a stress on the father, just as teaching the boy to ask for his needs was a stress to his mother. The father's desire to see his son grow, while enjoying his boy, provides the motivation to overcome this strain. Fathers who train their sons out of fear push them to perform and achieve, rather than teaching them to explore, express themselves and thereby find satisfaction in life.

Through this maze of confusion, it is the father who guides his son to satisfaction. Mother's milk was always satisfying, but the choices are not all good when a boy must decide what to feed himself. What does he choose and in what order?

Learning about food is just the beginning of making choices. What clothes should he wear? What friends should he choose? How should he spend his time? What is worth effort, suffering, or pain to obtain? What should be turned down even if it is immediately pleasurable because it is not satisfying? Father is one who can guide his steps and choices. In time his father will show him the difference between pleasure and satisfaction, and the boy will learn to make wise choices.

Finding satisfaction is a very important job. Without it, a boy will not be able to meet his needs. It takes a while to learn how to do this well. By the time he turns thirteen every boy should be fluent in what satisfies him, even when he must do hard things to find it.

Tragically, the majority of men do not appear to have finished the job of being a boy. Most of them do not know what they feel or how to meet their needs. This leaves them very vulnerable. When we are dissatisfied and do not know what satisfies us, we are sitting ducks for anyone who claims to have an answer.

Advertising, for example, is the fine art of creating dissatisfaction. The main purpose of most modern advertising is to create a feeling of dissatisfaction and then tell us what will meet that need. If we know what we need, there is no use advertising except to tell us where to find it. The popularity of advertising and the way most men succumb to it indicates that men have not finished being boys and do not know what satisfies their needs.

When Things Go Wrong

We can better understand the importance of a boy's bonds with his father when we look at what happens if they are missing or defective. The man who is not connected with his father does not trust other men. Furthermore, he does not trust his wife or daughter with other men either.

The man who has no bond with his father runs a great risk of becoming a conformist. He does not know how to be separate and make things happen. He is more prone to change than to cause changes. He is not in full possession of his own body. A father teaches a man to go after what he wants and to make things happen.

A weak bond with Dad produces a frantic search for both control and freedom. Such men need to get away from what they fear will control them. This kind of man fears commitment. Work and struggle pose a threat to him. He doesn't care who he hurts as he tries to escape. Rather than the courage from a connection to his father which tells him he can accomplish things, there is fear which leads to running away. Escape is necessary. He lacks the strength to get involved and stay involved. He runs away expending a great deal of energy to be free of any responsibilities.

God our Father says, "When you have done everything, stand." We don't have to run. He promises us the strength. We can go, we can do, we can be what is needed—we don't need to run. There is no need to frantically search for freedom.

I run sometimes. I remember one time a family fight broke out on an old subject. I quickly decided to go to the back bedroom to hide and pray. It was the perfect cover. I would gladly have prayed until everything was better, and I could go back out safely. God didn't like my using Him to escape my responsibility, so before long it became time to take a stand. I don't know that we resolved anything that day, but God prevailed in saying I needed to face the difficulty.

Sometimes a missing father keeps the boy from growing a bond. Other times a father will fail to be a good model. Each boy is the closest replica on earth of what his father is like. How he feels about his father will have a huge impact on how he sees himself. Even when he tries to be very different from his father, the boy is not free from the powerful influence of these feelings.

If a large oak tree drops an acorn, which grows into another oak tree, it will be a genetic replica of the original tree. Still, the effects of climate and disease may cause the two trees to grow very differently. In that sense the boy can be the closest replica of his father, although through the effects of his own climate he may grow in very different ways.

If we totally reject our fathers, we reject the model on which we were based. Such a rejection is a rejection of our very selves.

If someone were in a car accident and went through the windshield, we would not assume that what we found was what his face should look like. We know this because we know what our faces should look like, but we are not able to envision what evil does to people's souls.

To restore injured people, we must know what they were like before the injury. People with faces full of glass from the windshield will rightfully see themselves as ugly, but are they ugly? First we must take the glass out and stitch up their faces.

To stretch this analogy a bit, all of us have had our faces jammed through the windshield of sin and the world. We need our faces reconstructed by someone who knows what they should look like to begin with. A plastic surgeon would want a "before" picture. But since our world is thousands of years into the wreck, we have to go back to the Creator for a "before" picture. It is impossible to determine on our own what our lives would be without sin. We ask our heavenly Father to heal us so that we look like our father as God created him. In doing this we must come to terms with the fact that our father has no doubt been changed by sin and trauma.

At one point in my training, when I was being instructed in behavior modification, my services were requested to help a boy who was not doing well in school. We set up a program of goals he could reach. In return he received certain rewards. The reward the boy requested was to spend some time with his dad doing something fun. The father agreed and the standards for success were set. As a result the boy began to apply himself more diligently to his studies and earned all his points.

Two weeks later the family came in. The boy was worse than ever, so I asked what went wrong. The boy said, "I did everything, but my dad would not spend time with me."

I asked his father if this was true and he said, "Hey! That is how the world is! You don't always get what you expect. The kid just has to learn to live with that." The dad was happy, he thought he had just taught his son a valuable lesson. Now the boy would be like his father. Giving his son a scar like his own is how he saw being a good father. He needed to teach certain lessons the hard way. This is what happens when you don't have the eyes of heaven to see what someone ought to look like.

This father was well intentioned. There is a lot of training that occurs this way by those who don't know how to respond with love. Deep inside, men sense something wrong with the ways they relate to their own children. And yet, without the courage to face their own pain and their own losses, the trickle-down of cruelty is inevitable. Men, particularly those of this generation, must face the fact that the fathers and role models they seek are often not available. For this generation they must learn to give what they did not receive from their fathers. Unless we attempt to give, we will not grieve deeply. When we have grieved our losses, we can take the bits of life we have received to Jesus to multiply as he did the loaves and fishes. When this life is distributed by even a few faithful men, the love that is left over will be more than we started with. We will have life to give.

Fathers of Men

There have been times when my marriage has not been perfect. Some difficulties have lasted more than a few hours or even a few days. It was on one of those occasions that I called my dad. He wisely reminded me of my original intentions in marrying my wife.

I remember well the day that my dad first asked me about why I intended to marry so young. Did I know, he inquired, of the difficulties inherent in my selection of a mate? As we walked through the park at the edge of a beautiful lake we reviewed my life—past, present and future. Now, over the phone and fifteen years later he took me back to that park, the site of our talk. "You knew there would be tough times when you got married," he said, "and I seem to recall that you wanted the challenge."

My father's compassion was deeper than it appeared at first. We talked at some length about what it means to do things that are difficult and painful. Even though he did not particularly agree with me or support all that I was doing, my dad reminded me of my history, my commitments and most importantly, that there wasn't anything unmanly about working through difficulties.

A man's connection to his father goes on long beyond his father's death. Jesus taught that it was not what goes into a man that makes him unclean, but what comes out of his heart and mouth. A wise father will try to bring the best out of us, for he can see with the eyes of heaven what there is inside of us waiting to come out.

But what happens when a man has never learned what it means to be an infant or a boy—when the care and development provided by his parents has short-circuited?

4. THE MAN WHO HAS NEVER BEEN A BOY

Larry had the nicest house on the street. It wasn't the most expensive house, but everything about it was as close to perfect as Larry could get it. He worked on it at least four hours a night and twelve to sixteen hours a day on weekends. Larry had made many improvements in the six years he had owned the house.

Larry felt self-conscious about his home, because the neighbors teased him a bit, and his wife still seemed unhappy with his results. He could not decide what to do. Should he work more or less? Larry had a bad case of fear of disapproval. If you asked him why he worked so hard, he would tell you that he only wanted to be a good Christian husband and father. He tried to do what was expected of him by others and himself. Having never enjoyed his father's attention, he had become a man who had never been a boy.

The boy's job for his first twelve years is to learn how to take satisfactory care of himself. He is to learn how he feels and how to express these feelings so that they are understood. In doing these incredibly complex tasks, the boy learns what is truly satisfying and what is not.

The boy who is equipped in this way has learned what he likes from his mother's excellent attention and how to feed himself by his father's encouragement. He has become a part of his community and is recognized as such. This boy is ready to become a man.

The dysfunctional family is one in which the adults try to be children, while the children try to be adults. This inversion of roles is the best way of describing the effects of trying to be an adult without first learning the lessons of being a child. As we have also pointed out, these lessons are cumulative. Adult male development builds on a foundation of the child's development rather than replacing it.

Entitlement and Learning What You Can Produce

Entitlement

Perhaps the best way to describe the boy who has completed his training is to consider that the boy who has completed his infant tasks knows how to ask for what he needs. He considers himself to be entitled to have those needs met as a natural result of his existence. The boy who then has been trained well by his father knows how to ask for those things that satisfy and to avoid those that do not.

The sign of a complete boy is that he can ask for and receive what he needs with joy and without guilt or shame. While this will appear selfish to some, it is absolutely essential as a foundation for giving as an adult. The one who cannot receive freely cannot give freely.

Jesus, we are told, left his riches in heaven because he chose to do so. It is precisely because he knew he was under no obligation, guilt, or shame if he kept everything for himself that we can appreciate his gift.

In the trial of Ananias and Sapphira, the first Christians to receive the death penalty from God, a pivotal point by the prosecution was entitlement. "While it was in your hand, were you not free to do with it what you wanted?" asked the apostle Peter. He made it clear that giving was to be done freely. God, in fact, says that he does not want gifts given by compulsion, but he loves a cheerful giver. Only a man who has first been a boy can experience this truth. Perhaps this is part of why we cannot enter the kingdom of God unless we become as little children.

The problem for those who try to become men without first becoming boys is that they can only give if they are compelled to do so by shame, by guilt, or by fear. This becomes a good test for any man who wonders whether he has completed the task of being a boy. If you consider keeping your time, money, energy, or other resources for yourself, do you feel guilt and shame? If so, you have not learned entitlement. Do you experience guilt, shame, or embarrassment if someone gives something to you? If so, then you have not learned entitlement. The result is a loss of joy. The boy receives with joy. His food brings joy. His affection brings joy. His time brings joy. To the boy, receiving is joy. So it is that Solomon concluded his analysis of a man's life in Ecclesiastes by saying that everything beyond receiving what we need is emptiness (Eccl 8:15). A man who looks for joy elsewhere will not find it.

Solomon also points out that the other source of satisfaction for a man is to enjoy his work. The work of his hands, which comes out of him, satisfies. So, to Solomon, the tasks of the boy are the center of life, to receive your food, be loved, and to enjoy what you do.

Learning what you can produce

The man who learns to receive without learning what he can produce is also in a very bad place. He has indeed mastered the job of the infant child, but has not learned from his father to produce life. This man becomes an endless vacuum. Without guilt or shame, he will consume the world for himself. He feeds freely on all he can possess, and yet he is still not satisfied.

Consumption is not satisfying for a man. We must both take in and give out. The boy who has learned satisfaction from his father knows this well. He can see what satisfies and what does not. Consuming alone will never satisfy. The person who tries to reach satisfaction by consuming remains an infant doomed to consume in the vain hope that more will satisfy. This is what powers many addictions and especially takes root deeply in a consumer society. We are to believe that satisfaction will come from the resources we consume. More expensive is better. More is better. Buy and be satisfied. You are what you eat, or wear, or drive.

Entitlement without production will not satisfy. Some people fear that teaching their children that they are entitled to having their needs met and feelings respected will breed selfish children. Because such parents operate out of fear, they build guilt and shame in their children. These children never complete the task of childhood and so can never become adults that will give and receive freely and joyfully. There will always be "strings attached."

Most of the current trends on psychotherapy and popular psychology address this problem of the child within. They are secular attempts to find the kingdom through becoming like a child. They are correct in so far as they go. We must all be children first. The men's movement also affirms this need to be boys. Men who have not been boys have no roots with which to nourish the rest of their tree. They have far less support for the growth of their fruit.

Christians, on the other hand, have had a tendency to teach sacrificial giving at the expense of entitlement. In Sunday school they begin to teach that it is better to give than to receive, not because it is a step of maturity and therefore more gratifying, but because it is more "righteous" to give than to receive. Guilt then falls on any who prefer to receive or even who feel entitled to receive. This is the road to disaster.

A friend of mine tells a story which could be repeated by many a Christian child. His father had given him a new bicycle for his tenth birthday. A few weeks later a neighbor lost his car and needed transportation to get to work. Acting on the principle that it was more blessed to give than to receive, this father gave the bicycle to the neighbor. My friend was expected to be happier about this arrangement than he had been to receive the bicycle to begin with. Although he was old enough to understand the neighbor's plight and wanted to help, he could not get past the loss of his bicycle. Try as he might, my friend has never become happy about his loss. He continues to give and give, he even lives out of his car at times so he can give his children a private school education, but he is still not satisfied. Always haunting him is the feeling that he has lost what is precious to him.

Now, don't get me wrong. It was not losing the bicycle that made him live in a car. These are only symptoms of a boy who never learned entitlement. He is nearly a saint by some standards, but he lacks joy. He became a man without completing his work as a boy.

Three Mistakes Wounded Men Make

The three classic mistakes of a man who has not learned to be a boy are to try to gain value or satisfaction by consuming, to seek value or satisfaction through action, and to proceed through life following some set of guidelines, without seeing if they bring him any satisfaction. Any boy could do better than these wounded men.

The Consumer

Bill was meticulous about his clothes. Bill shopped at the right stores and drove a BMW with a great stereo system. Never one to be ostentatious, Bill was understated but always had the right wine for the occasion, the house in the right neighborhood, and just the right friends. Although he was only "worth" $750,000, many of his friends were millionaires.

Bill left his wife for a younger woman. He left his job for one with more prestige and financial security that let him spend his days with the very wealthy. He moved into a new house with his new wife in a better neighborhood and had new kids. He left his old friends for better ones who didn't ask about his ex-wife or kids. Bill now throws bigger parties for more people, has replaced his old BMW with a new one, has a faster computer, manages a larger staff, and eats in finer restaurants.

Bill even traded in his doctor for a new one. It seems that some of the nurses in the doctor's office were becoming amused by Bill's endless stream of worries about his body and his health. His doctor could find nothing wrong that merited treatment, even though Bill's tennis game was declining a bit. He fastidiously moved to healthier and healthier foods.

Bill did eventually go to see a therapist. The doctor was a prominent professor and owned several counseling centers. As Bill commented, the doctor charged top fee. Bill didn't see the need to stay long. Bill was consumed with consuming. What he could not consume he stored for later consumption. Bill had reached the American dream, but few people I knew respected him as a man. He seemed to think his value came from his possessions.

The Doer

Some men take their value from what they do. Sam said he would never retire. He loved construction. At six every morning, seven days a week he found himself at the pancake house with the other contractors swapping stories and subcontracts. His truck and his tools went everywhere he did. Sam worked until late afternoon most days and took pride in his work.

Sam's wife had a life of her own and told a few of her friends that Sam just watched TV and was unpleasant at home. So she didn't care that he was still working at age sixty-nine.

Sam took a vacation one time with a friend and set off to see the country, but they had a disagreement early in the trip. His friend nearly left him in a café to let him find his own way home. Sam was not much for conversation unless he was able to talk about his work.

When Sam had a heart attack and found he could not work, he became miserable. He told everyone that all he wanted to do was die.

Sam was a contractor. It wasn't just because he built things that he had become a contractor. What he built was who he was. To see his finished work was to see himself. Aside from what he did, Sam was not able to recognize himself. Sam thought his value came from what he could produce.

The Rule-maker

Paul was as dutiful a pastor as any church board would ever hope to find. He was a man of experience, principle, commitment, and virtue. He did not lack compassion for his congregation and visited both the weak and strong. Paul was a man of vision and with his help churches grew. As an excellent pastor, he taught and studied carefully, but he allowed no room for change or uncertainty.

Paul was also a family man. He loved his wife and three children. Paul even loved the family dog. One day Paul came to see me because he was not sure whether to continue as a pastor. Something was wrong, and he couldn't quite put his finger on what it was. Because he was a man of high principle, he needed to find out what was wrong, why his work seemed to be unfulfilling.

Paul's father was a pastor. His parents cared for him and never abused him. His family had taught Paul all the right things. Paul knew how to evaluate, solve problems, and do what was right. In seminary Paul even improved on the things his family had taught him, but there was one thing Paul did not know. Paul had no idea what satisfied him. He did not even realize that he should know what would satisfy him. Somehow, asking what satisfied him seemed "fleshly" and wrong, a bit too selfish.

Living without knowing what really satisfied him had almost ruined him. Paul had too many right choices every morning and no way to know which of them brought him life. He needed to learn to choose.

Without knowing which of these things brought satisfaction, Paul could only continue to review his principles and set priorities, but it troubled him that so many good things *never* got done. In time his energy waned and he began to dread his work. "Perhaps," he reasoned, "I am not meant to be a pastor, or I would have joy in my life."

This pastor knew that his value did not come from his work or from what he possessed. He lost interest in his work because as a human being he needed to be satisfied by his labor and food, but he had no hint on how to choose wisely. His father before him had not known what satisfied and never thought to teach his son. As a result, they would both continue until they collapsed from exhaustion and wonder where the time had flown. Satisfaction is the emotional fuel that keeps us running to meet the next challenge we face.

Between Bill, who tries to be a man by consuming, Sam, who is obsessed with his work, and Paul, who has lost his way, we see a few of the pitfalls of trying to be a man without first becoming a boy.

Men have been trying to heal this wounded boy for some time. The "liberated man" who, in response to the women's movement, learned to feel and need, has learned one-third of the job of being a boy. If he thought this would please the women around him, he was wrong. In learning to be sensitive, he has become an infant and learned only what a mother would teach him about being a baby. Women want a man, not just an infant, and not a mama's boy. If he has also learned entitlement and to produce from himself, then he will have something to give. He now knows two-thirds of what a boy should know. The final third of being a boy only comes from learning what truly satisfies. The boy who has learned all these things is ready to become a man. Although he will not live only to satisfy women, he can become the man women seek.

Meanwhile, during the last two decades, the so-called liberated yuppie women, have been learning how to produce. They have learned two-thirds of being a girl: they can feel and they can do, though many have yet to learn what truly satisfies. Many too have found they have large defects in their ability to feel and are now taking care of their own inner child. This kind of a woman does not satisfy a man looking for a woman and not a girl.

Trying to be a man without first being a boy is very discouraging. In the end, the impostor will be found out because he will consume too much or too little, work too much or too little, and never be satisfied. He will run out of strength just when he needs it, like the foolish virgins who ran out of light because they did not buy enough oil for their lamps.

Men who do not know how to be boys will fall asleep behind the wheel, because they didn't believe they needed sleep. They will believe the billboard that shows a glass of whiskey and the caption, "What a successful executive earns in a day." It will be a life of pain, as they fail to ask and so fail to receive. As pretenders to the throne, they demand in fear what they would freely be given in love. At the same time they flee the power wielded by those entitled to possess and give.

Given this woundedness in the lives of so many men, we now need to explore what it means to become a man. There are just too many wounded little boys walking around in men's bodies wondering whether anyone will ever show them what it really means to be a man.

III. A MAN

5. Becoming a Man

The men at the retreat gather in small circles of eight to twelve. The oldest man in the circle stands up. He goes from man to man in the circle, placing his hands on their shoulders and proclaiming this simple blessing: "God, your Father, loves you. This day I declare in his name that you are a man. God is very pleased."

The men tremble as tears well up in their eyes. They let the words sink in. In hushed tones they speak haltingly. At every retreat it is the same. Men of all ages hear for the first time that they are men, and this is pleasing to God. Invariably, this simple ceremony becomes the highlight of the retreats I lead.

Joel was a strong man with a firm handshake. He had a look about him that gave the impression that he usually got his way. As he sat down, he informed us that he was a retired fighter pilot and father of three grown children.

"I want to become a man. When I am with men, even those who are years my junior, I feel like a boy inside. That is why I came." Joel's words were clear, as he looked at the eyes of each man in the circle.

Larry sat back in his chair, his legs straight ahead of him. "I am a federal marshal and the father of three children. I'm always afraid that I'll do something wrong and get yelled at. If anyone gets mad at me I feel like a little boy. I worry constantly."

Larry and Joel were waiting for the moment when they would feel like men inside. They were both approaching retirement. They felt loss and shame because what they thought would happen never did.

Other men spoke up. They had hoped that getting a wife, having a successful career, or landing a promotion might make them feel like men. That didn't work either. They turned to the older men waiting to hear the words they had never heard, "You are a man."

Joel was first. He was the oldest in the group. After he had blessed the other men, they placed their hands on his head. At last he heard what every thirteen-year-old boy needs to hear from his dad and the men of his community. Only, for Joel it had taken an extra forty years.

This blessing of being called to manhood launches a boy on his next great adventure—an adventure with real consequences, responsibilities, and costs, because this is real life. This is his life.

Suppose we have a healthy thirteen-year-old boy who knows what he feels and is able to express his feelings clearly. He also knows what he needs and what will satisfy him. He knows how to ask for help when he needs it. The boy knows he is of great value because God has said so. Yet the boy knows there is more to life than he has experienced. Men seem to have a power with each other that is out of range to him. He senses the pressure when men collide, yet like mountain rams, they walk away unharmed. He is about to discover a new meaning for a word he has known since kindergarten—fairness.

"It's not fair," screams the child.

"We shall make it fair," says the man.

Manhood is all about fairness. The evolving male is now responsible to look out for his neighbor's needs in the same way he has looked out for his own. He can satisfy two or more people at once. For the child, "it's not fair" means his own needs and feelings were ignored. For the man, "it's not fair" means the needs and feelings of others are not to be ignored. The boy, up to this point, has had to meet his own needs, seek his own satisfaction. He now faces his first major challenge. His actions now will have an impact on others for whom he has assumed responsibility. To be a man means the needs of others are given the same consideration as his own. If this does not happen, a man will not be satisfied himself and his contribution to history will be marred. A man must love his neighbor as himself. Fair is fair.

A Man Is a Part of History

For the normal boy the step into manhood is an awesome discovery. He becomes a part of history. Because he has lived, life will not be the same for other people, whether it be for good or for ill. His father and the men who know their own history will instruct him. Since the normal boy understands satisfaction, he immediately wants to know what participation in history will be the most satisfying for him. By learning these secrets, he will become a wise, good man.

Perhaps it is not right to call the means of participating in history "secrets," because they are so plainly seen. But to the untrained eye they may appear as secrets. By examining past history, the boy learns of history yet to come. Since the thirteen-year-old is not skilled at seeing large patterns, he must first hear the history of his own family and people, his own town and life. If he first understands what is nearby, he will then grasp what is far away. The true stories of how he came to be, who he his, and how through him others will come to be who they are, are the stories that make a man.

A man knows too that "his-story" is only a part of history. Not only his interests but also those of others are to be fairly represented. At thirteen the new man begins to think, "What is fair? What can I do to meet the needs of others and my own as well?"

Redemptive History

For the Christian all history is redemptive. That can be painful because the truth about us is often ugly. But men must handle the pain of knowing the truth, whether it hurts or not. If it hurts, they must learn to grieve.

Being a part of history is important. What we do begins to matter. Who we are matters a great deal. All of history is an ongoing fight. We are participants whether we want to be or not.

Listen to the story that every new man must know:

God created the world. To the two people he put in charge he said, "This is a wonderful garden, but it may become infected by a very nasty virus. I have sworn to get rid of that virus. As I live, I will wipe it out. Only good will be eternal. Evil will not survive. Anything that gets contaminated by the virus will be wiped out too. I have determined to get rid of both the virus and its influence. Don't mess with the virus. As soon as you do, you'll be on my list of things that have been infected and will not be eternal."

Adam said one day, "Excuse me, Lord God, I noticed that there are two kinds of animals. But there is only one kind of me. I like petting the kitten, playing with the dog, riding the horse, hugging the koala, laughing with the otter, and talking to the parrot, but could I put in a request for another one like me?"

And God said, "I like your idea. I will do just that." And God created woman. Adam took his problem to God. God said, "I like your idea. We'll work on it together." They did and it was better than before.

We can still do that. We have an idea, we can take it to the Lord and say, "Can you do something about it?" And God says, "What a good point you have! I like working on history with you." And so we talk it over until we have a plan.

Back in the garden, however, someone pointed out another problem to Adam, "Say! You guys don't know the difference between good and evil. There is a tree over here with the answers to all your problems." And so the tree that was supposed to point to God became a god, the first of many. Men began to carve trees for gods, until they finally used one to try to kill God himself. Trying to decide good and evil for ourselves let in the virus.

Adam had his influence on history. Because of that we all got infected and are all scheduled for elimination. God will not tolerate evil to be eternal. Therefore he provided a decontamination process. This would cost us our bodies. But he will give us new bodies after decontamination. God said he would take us from glory unto glory. He makes the good even better. This is the history we help create.

Every man should know this story. The snake would like us to forget about our part in history. He would like us to believe that we only play a negative role. Then, we go back to acting like little boys who are only concerned about themselves. The problems arise when these "little boys" inside men's bodies start running homes, churches, and businesses with the goal of avoiding pain themselves.

The Bible has long stories about these "boys" who didn't know or care that they were making history and set off instead to find pleasure and avoid pain. Yet God stays involved with history in order to redeem it. He can do that two ways: by stamping out evil or by redeeming us and our history with us. We need not fear our pain, shame, or ugliness, for God can and will see us through to a glorious end. He can take the worst situation and redeem it. We are God's witnesses and the bearers of hope that decontamination from the virus of sin is a reality.

Our stories are our histories. There is no changing them for they have made us what we are. When men come to me for counseling I ask them to write an autobiography going back to the time before birth. Then we focus on preschool years, grade school, junior high, high school, college or career starts, marriage, and on into the present. We look for the hurts in their lives and prayerfully ask for the healing of those hurts. We also talk about the pain the man has caused others, for hurt people cannot help but hurt others. By sharing these stories with their friends, wives and children, men become at last a part of redemptive history. They know they are men with a story worth telling.

Yet even as men claim their own part in redemptive history, they need to be aware of three killer myths in modern society that threaten to enslave them. We tackle these next.

Myths

Myth One—Men Can't Handle the Truth

Somewhere in the mid-seventies writers began to take notice of men. They wrote about the "fragile male ego." For the first time men were allowed to have needs. They are not the rocks they appear to be, for inside they have needs and feelings just like women.

To this day many men think sex is all they really need. They have grown up in a culture that denies men have emotional needs. They aren't even allowed to need sleep. Men have had to create euphemisms to talk about sleep. "I've got to hit the sack," or "catch a little shut eye," anything but say, "I need sleep. I'm tired." Real men don't admit needing sleep, let alone anything else. Little wonder that many men do not operate well. The fragile male ego finally made room for a man to have needs and feelings, even if he did not know how to say, "I need to go to sleep." Women had to understand that when men growled they really meant, "I'm tired."

What came along with the fragile ego was a fear of telling men the truth about themselves. You can't tell a man the truth if you are hurting his feelings. Since men were known to retreat from the onslaught of feelings and words into silent or angry pain, the myth of the fragile male ego was born, in other words "men can't take the truth." You can't tell him he is messing up his family or being irresponsible at work. He can't handle it. His ego might break.

When we can't tell the truth, we can't be part of real life. We can't know our part in history. We can't even begin to measure our impact. We can't know who we are and what we do if we don't start with the truth. As a result, there are a lot of men who are confused and don't know how much pain they can handle. We simply "stuff" it.

Myth Two—Men Shouldn't Show Pain

Men have the strength to experience pain, but rather than face the grief of World War I and World War II, Korea, Vietnam, genocide, oppression, and lost fathers, showing no pain became a way to prove their masculinity. Gangs, cold war spies, and tough guys relied on this test of manhood. Tribal initiations, high school football, and boot camps sometimes use this test as well.

Instead of learning that men can survive pain and need not fear it, men began to think that enduring pain without showing it was manly. These stoic fathers produced sons who often assumed that if their father didn't show pain he felt nothing.

Men who do not speak honestly about pain will never know how much they can take. What began as strength ended as deception. A man may feel that he can handle physical pain, especially if it is inflicted on a football field. But can he handle the pain of feeling sad, sad, sad—so sad that it would make him cry?

Did we ever see our fathers facing emotional pain, going through it, and teaching us, "You know, son, this will hurt, but we can take it"? Only rarely. They were simply silent, even detached about it, or, they stupidly suffered unnecessary pain because admitting pain might make them unmanly. Truth is often painful, so rather than greeting silence men retreat to the shelter of the fragile male ego or the suffering, silent stone.

Yet all of us know the moment will come when we must face the truth about ourselves, and say, "This is going to hurt." If we really look at ourselves, there is a good chance something is going to be ugly. It is painful to be ugly. If we are honest every man has to say, "I've done something ugly," or, "There is something wrong with me. If I look at how I grew up, there is going to be something ugly there too. What will I do with that pain? Will it destroy me? Will it alter me so that I won't ever be a man? Will I show pain in front of other guys? Will I still be a man if I feel emotional pain?"

The alternate strategy is for men to avoid feeling pain entirely. This means that all pain has to be borne by someone else. Perhaps this is a good definition of evil: the result of making others bear our pain. Such men try to take control, because if they are in control, they don't have to feel pain.

Recently I was in the store and observed a four-year-old boy acting up. The boy embarrassed his dad by making a scene, so the dad reacted. His father hit him, then hit him again, saying, "Shut up, or I'm going to give you something to really cry about!" Everyone was going to see that he knew how to control his son. It was a power struggle right to the end. The dad was not going to be embarrassed and feel any emotional pain. If anyone was going to feel pain, it would be the son. No matter how much power it took, the father would use all he needed to be in control and avoid the pain. Actually the only pain for the father was embarrassment, but he was not even going to accept that.

Myth Three—A Man Should Always Be in Control

Staying in control is perhaps the main method used by men or women to avoid feeling pain of any kind. The person in control can ostensibly make events turn out in ways that avoid discomfort to oneself. Two of the favorite ways are using threats and blaming people:

Jesus never threatened anyone, as we read in 1 Peter 2:23, "When he suffered, he made no threats." In fact people cannot be controlled. God gave both children and adults free will which he does not take away just because we don't behave. Although Jesus experienced extreme pain, he did not threaten or blame.

Anytime we try to control something that can't be controlled, it will make us feel out of control. A man can't control his girlfriend, wife, children, employees, or anyone else. He may hope to influence them in a positive manner, but he can't control them. Not even God controls them. He had two children whom He put in a garden. They blew it.

Blame is deciding whose fault it is. When things went wrong in the Garden of Eden, God did not ask whose fault it was. He only wanted to know, "What happened here?" God is interested in truth. The man's answer was blaming or accusatory, "It is her fault."

Adam's ego was not too fragile for God to ferret out the truth. What did happen here? This is the question God wants every man to ask about his own life. Men who ignore this end up in the category the Bible calls fools. Fools are those who try to avoid pain and control other people. The man who has to control has never learned to trust.

The signs of a fool are: they are always right; they slander (blame) their family; they try to have everything their way so that nothing bothers or hurts them.

Jesus did not run away from suffering. We are promised this same strength as men.

Even if we have never survived pain before, or had the courage to really face it, we can find the strength if we are willing to face the truth. It is only when we are honest about ourselves that we can begin to know our place in history. A man is someone who becomes a part of history.

Men will never begin to make sense of life until they admit that the games they play are ways to avoid the pain they claim they don't feel.

How Sons Become Men

Many men have no idea when or how they came to be men. Just as it took them years to become boys, so it will take young men many years to become men in the fullest sense.

When, after more than four thousand hours of practice, I was granted my license as a psychologist, I felt very shaky about being on my own. I was a psychologist, but I knew there was much I still had to learn. In the same way, a thirteen-year-old boy becomes a man, but he knows that most of what it means to be a man is yet to be learned.

The boy who passes his thirteenth year without recognition, without a rite of passage, begins to feel the internal tension of being a man. He has no idea of how to proceed. He is left on his own and at the mercy of his peers to invent a way to be recognized as a man. In fact, men often take very circuitous routes to prove they are really men. When I took scuba diving lessons, I had a chance to see how men aboard dive boats proved to others that they were really men.

On board dive boats, there was a simple and often repeated ritual among men who were meeting for the first time. This simple test of masculinity required only three comments—two about women and one about men. Upon meeting, the men would talk briefly about diving. Then the man who had first approached the other would make a crude sexual remark about women and how much he liked them. Typically, he would follow that up with a gay-bashing comment and conclude with another demeaning sexual remark about women. Now that their manliness had been established, the men could talk more about diving, be friendly with each other, and ask one another about equipment. Just about every man on the boat seemed to follow this formula. It made me wonder, since I wanted to dive, how I might make it as a man since I can't stomach insulting homosexuals or crude comments about women.

Gordon Dalbey suggests in his book, Father and Son, that the great struggle to separate a boy from his mother and unite him with the community of men is what ushers a boy into manhood. He calls this experience the "rite of passage."

I see this rite as a passage from boyhood into manhood. It is, in fact, the first conscious identity shift that a male will experience. Unlike his weaning, this time he goes into the crucible of change with his eyes open, but not knowing who he will become. Strengthened by the community of men and the confidence of both his parents, the boy undertakes the scariest of all journeys. He leaves the security of his known sense of self as a boy for a new, unknown identity as a man. Once a boy has made this journey, there will be no overwhelming fear when God calls him to new identities later in life. Once he has made the journey from one identity to a greater one, he realizes that he can survive the passage into the unknown.

God transforms us "from glory to glory" in a series of identity changes throughout our lifetime--unless fear stops us from changing. Each time, we leave behind the comfort and restriction of knowing who we are for the greater glory of becoming someone we do not yet understand. Those who have experienced a rite of passage from boyhood to manhood will understand God's excitement at taking us on a journey, even though we never know the outcome in advance.

Although it may not be apparent at first, the passage into young manhood is the first real preparation for death—for the father first and then for the son. In death, all that one knows ceases to exist, and a transformation takes place. We assume a new identity in a brand-new kind of existence. In facing this major step into young manhood, the boy makes the transition to a new identity in the company of men and his family. He learns that a man can survive and face the unknown challenge he must one day confront alone at death. And yet he is not alone, for he is surrounded by a "great crowd of witnesses." The rite of passage reduces our eventual fear of death. We have survived one passage and can survive others. We move from glory to glory.

I believe that a boy who had his father's involvement to lead him from the infant to child stage will not have an identity dominated by his mother. Therefore, there should be no further need for the son to separate from the mother when he becomes a man. In his great leap to become someone more glorious than a boy, he will naturally want the support of both parents and the wider community. A boy raised by his father to express what is inside himself and seek satisfaction in his efforts will not be in for a great struggle. The normal transition into manhood may look something like the following.

How a Boy Becomes a Man

A Time of Preparation

The preparations for manhood begin long before the boy turns thirteen. Each boy has already been through two transitions. The first is his birth, where his mother is the principle player. He has often been told of this great day and each year his birthday has been celebrated. His second transition required his help as he joined his father at the feast of his weaning and put food into his own mouth. These two transitions, achieved and frequently reviewed, foreshadow still greater changes ahead.

Previews of their adult identity occur when boys see how men behave. Some boys watch their fathers at home or go with them on trips to the store. Other boys see men on television, visit Grandpa, or watch men at church, parks, and family gatherings. The boy knows that he will become a man at the appointed time, so he does not have to interrupt childhood by trying to prove he is a man when he isn't.

Groups of boys can prepare together through a church or when several families band together. Groups like Squires of the Cross begin teaching the values men require to eight to ten year old boys. Individual preparation and mentoring by both parents and men from the community becomes more important as boys reach twelve years of age. The objective is to prepare the self centered boy for the day he will serve a Lord and a purpose greater than himself. The final year of preparation should help determine when each boy is really ready to become a man. The ceremonial time should match the boy's readiness.

A Rite of Passage

The ceremony should have three parts. There is a private examination of the boy by his father and men he trusts to be sure of the boy's healing, spiritual state, commitment to sexual and personal purity. A second aspect of the rite of passage is for males only and involves acceptance into the fellowship of men as one of them. The third part of the ceremony should be celebrated and commemorated with symbols, and ceremonies. There is some debate over whether this ceremony should be done individually for each boy or for a group of boys together. Both kinds of ceremonies seem to serve the purpose, provided that each boy is individually ready and that following the ceremony the young man becomes part of a group of young men with whom he can develop a life-giving group identity.

The initiation or rite of passage means a change of identity, for the boy is no longer a child but now a man. Although it is frightening to leave behind one's identity in search of another, there is comfort and support in the company of those who have already made the journey and those who are making it with him. Thirteen is a great year.

A mother's pride, encouragement, and natural concerns help the newly initiated youth experience that for women being a man is a good thing. This keeps the boyhood gains alive as the man grows. Without this balance, new growth might crowd out the old, leaving the man to wither. Just because you are a man doesn't mean you don't need your oatmeal!

A Time of Formation

The training in manliness starts in earnest as the young man receives his first roles in the community of men. Even though he practiced arguing over baseball rules in grade school, his first roles as a man are unglamorous opportunities to assist and observe men negotiating and working out problems to everyone's advantage.

The community insures that time and resources are available for young adults to form a cohesive group of peers. This group identity prepares the way for skilful participation with older adults. It helps them develop their personal style. The peer group also helps form the basis for social, educational, work and ultimately marriage relationships.

Older men will frequently ask the question of two young men, "What will satisfy you both?" and expect the young men to work out their own arrangements with each other. By modeling and encouragement, they will teach the fledgling men to take pride in fairness by bargaining strenuously. The older men pay attention to the beginners' progress and help them see the needs of others and thus avoid abuse of power.

For young men, participation in their new group identity often springs from the normal activities of life. Something as basic as hospitality and making sure that everyone is fed and able to participate in activities is a simple start. Young men who are looking for jobs learn fairness by negotiating the payment for mowing a lawn, painting a garage, or taking pictures for the neighbors' fiftieth anniversary.

More important, however, are the opportunities supplied by older men. Asking a young man's opinion and participation in discussions and decisions is very valuable training. Very often the men of the church will plan to help someone who is sick, invalid, abandoned, or impoverished. Younger men can be actively involved in taking inventory of needs, planning what has to be done, or even taking charge of parts of the project that fit their skills. For example, they make sure that all the watering and weeding is done in an invalid's yard. Young men are not cheap labor. They need to be part of the decision-making by the men, such as who will help this week and why.

This can be accomplished in the family by asking the young man to help plan his portion of the family budget, and who to include on family trips, vacations, holidays, and other activities. Planning activities that reach out to neighborhood children who lack stable homes or the lonely and elderly can help the young man balance his own needs with those of people who do not have the same resources.

Sometimes a young man can be selected for a special task in order to help train him. Greg was picked by his father to choose the right site and boat rental for the men's fishing trip his dad was scheduled to lead. He helped Greg list the different features and advantages he needed so he could compare boats. Then he let his son call, negotiate, and finally select the best boat and site for the trip. It took a lot of time, more time than it would have taken his dad, but the training and sense of accomplishment that Greg experienced when he headed out with the men made it worthwhile.

Winging It

Solo flight arrives within five years of becoming a man. The independence and confidence developed among the community of men and from one's own family soon require decisions and consequences to rest on the young man's shoulders. The next step may be finding a job. It may mean moving into an apartment or going away to college. Solo flight usually involves making decisions like buying a car and other financial considerations such as deciding when to spend, save, or borrow money. In fact, deciding where you will work or who will be your roommate when you rent are part of the risks in taking responsibility for your own life. The soloist must decide when to ask for help and advice and what mistakes or losses are tolerable. Solo flight is never accomplished completely alone.

Simon was a junior in advanced placement classes when he decided to exercise the option of skipping his senior year and enter college early. He had many ideas of what to do with his life, which in one way means that he had no idea what to do. Simon had started taking evening classes in junior college in order to learn Japanese. Instead of giving a graduation present, he asked his parents to send him on a trip to Japan. After careful consideration as a family, it was decided that he and two friends would take a seven-week trip through Japan.

It was a sacrifice on the part of the parents to send him there, but more importantly they wanted him to see what it was like in other cultures.

To make the trip work, Simon had to plan it with the help of many people. Friends of the family and other parents helped Simon figure out transportation, lodging, food, and other needs for each day of the trip. When he actually arrived, he discovered that traveling in Japan, living in Japanese homes, and experiencing minority status left him constantly in need of negotiating what was good for him, his traveling companions, his hosts, and the friends he made.

When he returned home and started college, Simon was a changed man. His appreciation for his family, friends, and the help of others was greatly increased. Simon sought counsel from older men about career choices, changes in majors, and schools. He looked out for the needs of his friends and roommates as well as his own. Unlike many other college students, he loved to call home and tell his parents what he was doing and receive both their advice and admiration. In addition, he continued to discover what was satisfying for him and what was not. From calculus to aquariums, bicycles to sushi, sleeping with the window open to helping people escape cults, Simon examined it all. He was winging it.

But whether the soloist succeeds completely or not, his results are part of the family history to be applauded, analyzed, and in time refined for future flights. The young man expresses his feelings and explores his needs in discussions about what satisfied him and what didn't. Thus he begins to understand the impact and benefits of his achievement for himself and others.

Fatherhood is on the horizon.

6. LIFE-GIVING MEN

"Men exist to fight wars and open the lids on jars"

Ralph M.

"I used to think I needed a man to get things off the top shelf, but now I have a stepladder."

Elsie B.

For the first eight years that I was a counselor, I saw mostly women. Most of them came in to tell me how bad men were and how they hated them. Then one day they would notice I was there and say, "But not you, of course." Eventually I tried to hide my masculinity because I didn't really want them to know I was a man.

When dealing with disgruntled women, instead of being a man I was a "therapist," whatever that is. Indeed I was ashamed of what men had done and didn't want to be seen as a representative of all that hurtful and evil behavior.

For rather a long time, it hasn't been popular to be a man, although the men's movement has begun to turn that around. In fact, being a man and in particular a father, has been considered so unimportant that I never had a course, not even a lecture, on the subject in any of my four years of college and six years of graduate school. Perhaps it is this disregard and hostility that has led to the men's movement in the 1990s.

Two factors changed my secret shame of being a man and changed my counseling caseload from mostly women to mostly men. The first of these revelations came from the community of men and the second from a special group of women. Both showed the same miraculous truth: men have something good to offer.

The first factor was seeing my name on a who's who list of fathering advocates in America. Not that I was impressed with myself as a father, but when Ken Canfield of the National Center for Fathering spoke of the fathering guilt that even good fathers carry, it occurred to me that having regrets did not make me all bad. Being a father was indeed good. In fact, I had been and was good for my sons, as well as for other men who had experienced a father deficit.

The second factor that took away my secret shame for being a man came from women. Several women who read my book about fathering told me that they would have liked to have me as their father. These women were incest survivors, some of them the very ones who had been so vitriolic about men earlier. The truth slowly sunk in. Being a man was good. Men were to be a source of life, protectors of what is good. There is no shame in that! It is not something that men do from time to time, but the very essence of what they are created to become.

Men began to seek me out, asking to be taught this secret. For the first time in my life I was really glad to be a man. To be what one is, *is* good—splendid, even. I represented good news to other men, because good news is what I was created to be, just as is everyone else.

With this new appreciation for myself, I began to develop my own flair for life. As men become men, their wobbly efforts begin to demonstrate a sense of style. Without this joyful self-expression, men become merely functionaries, doers, and conveniences for others, as the quotes at the beginning of the chapter indicate. Yes, Ralph, men protect and serve, but they are also lovers. Lovers develop a style to please the senses of their beloved. Yes, Elsie, men have bodies, bodies that sustain their needs. They are not only there to reach the top shelf, but they are also servants. The servant attends to details and the manner in which he serves. He does not simply perform service, but service flows from him expressed in his own unique style for the enjoyment of those served as well as himself.

Particularly in our consumer society, it is important to know that men have something to offer. A young man who possesses this knowledge will view all his actions and relationships differently. He knows himself to be a brother, friend, warrior, lover, servant, and even a source of life. All of these sides of his identity come to be expressed with a style that is uniquely his own. Whether he pursues marriage, schooling, or work, the contented, satisfied man is the one who knows that owning and consuming do not make him a man. It is not having pretty women and fast cars but receiving and giving life that bring joy. In the many roles of his life, a man can experience the goodness of being male.

Man As Brother

The identity of a man as a brother is one that carries over from childhood. Boys learn to be brothers. Then as men they learn to expand this type of relationship beyond the biological family. This is to say that men have brotherly relationships with an expanding number of people. This component of a man's identity contributes greatly to his sense of fairness. A brother learns, long before he becomes a man, that the needs and feelings of his siblings matter. His entire family will have taken pains to point this out. Yet with siblings there is often a note of competition, or perhaps even the feeling that there isn't enough to go around. In the man this must be corrected. Each man must know in his heart that there is enough goodness for everyone so that he will always pursue the common good.

Dating is one extension of the brother role into the female world. In the great love poem, the Song of Solomon, the king refers to his beloved as his sister, "You have stolen my heart, my sister, my bride" (4:9). Perhaps this is not the average red-blooded American boy's dream, but I'm not too impressed with the average romance and marriage in our day. We would do far better to approach our dates as sisters than as mere entertainment for our viewing pleasure.

When I was dating, I noticed that most of the girls I dated were mad at the boy they had dated before me. Often he had taken liberties with her feelings or her body that had hurt her. Knowing that someday I would be marrying one of these girls caused me to wonder in what shape I would like my bride to be when I received her. The Golden Rule, "Do unto others as you would have them do unto you," took on practical meaning. My dating goal, which I also taught to my sons, was to treat a girl in such a way that were I ever to meet the husband of a girl I had dated, he would want to shake my hand and thank me.

Man as Friend

Being a friend, just like being a brother, is another component that boys carry over into manhood. Like brotherhood, friendship develops with age. As he matures, a man has more depth to bring friendship. It is a relationship for all seasons. For children, friendship provides a crucial source of comparison with others that is necessary for identity to form correctly. Children spend considerable effort comparing everything about themselves with others. While such comparisons can be used destructively, their healthy use is necessary for proper development. Friends are the yardsticks against which we measure ourselves. People tend to find yardsticks about their own size to measure themselves.

Friendships also help children learn to appreciate people who are different from themselves. Men need friends for both stretching and measuring. Men need friends for fun. Friends are the greatest help in developing a personal style, for they help us know how to express the things that make us uniquely ourselves and point out when that uniqueness is offensive. A man will often develop a style that complements his friends' styles. That can be good or bad, but the man without friends is usually an offense to eyes, ears, and nose.

It's worth noting, however, that American men typically have a problem developing deep and lasting friendships, particularly with fellow men. The lack of close friendships among men has been attributed to many factors. I believe that for most men their avoidance of close relationships with other males really stems from an unspoken fear of rejection by the male subculture, which is characterized by insulting and slightly hostile repartee. In common parlance, men refer to it as "just kidding around," under the cover of harmless banter about such things as sports, sex, fast cars, and the news. The hostility and insults usually come in the form of "put-downs" of newcomers and anyone who is different.

Man as Priest

The priest keeps things covered—not covered up, but covered. Men find joy in covering. The consumer believes that there is satisfaction in uncovering, in "Take it off." But the priest keeps things covered. He has no room for gossip, tales, and the rumors that keep *People* magazine, the talk shows, and crime shows in business. He knows the difference between discovery and exploitation.

The priest keeps things covered, but not through denial. He practices intercession both before God and with those who need to learn mercy and forgiveness. The priest keeps the channels clear and the good faith between people flowing. The priest never diminishes the size of a sin, but seeks to increase the size of the repentance and mercy. By making sure that each infraction is forgiven and cleansed, the priest covers. The priest wants history to be spotless and clean so that God's decontamination will be complete. To this end, each priest adds his own style and flair. Men find covering very satisfying.

Man as Lover

"Love covers a multitude of sins," Scripture tells us. Man as a lover is in harmony with man as a priest because both cover. In a limited sense, being a lover can refer to a man's sexual passion, but the lover is much more than sexual in his love of the beloved. The strength of love highlights each man's style perhaps more than any other role. The greatest attribute of the lover is his fearlessness. The Scripture says, "Perfect love casts out fear." The lover is even more fearless than the warrior.

The lover is known by whom and what he loves. The good lover loves the giver more than the gift, God more than life, the woman more than sex, the child more than the results. The lover celebrates life without fear, freely giving life and strength to others. The lover pursues, embraces, laughs, releases, and then pursues again. In all these movements, he includes the elements of his own style that will please him and his loves. The man is lover to boy and girl, grandmother and grandfather, dog and cat, and in time, his bride and wife.

The boy cannot be a lover because he thinks too much of his own needs, feelings, and satisfaction. A man is set free to be a lover because he can appreciate both his own feelings and those of his love.

Man as Warrior

The men's movement has brought with it the return of the warrior, this time not as a destroyer but as a defender, like the heroic warrior in epic stories and poems. But clever as Ulysses was with the Cyclops and inspiring as the myths can be, author Gordon Dalbey probably got closer to the truth when he said that the warrior carries the sword of truth.

Ultimately the warrior knows that there are things more important than his own life, of a value greater than himself. The warrior ultimately seeks a people and a king or prophet to outlive him should his own life be lost in the struggle for what is greater then himself. The boy will always seek his own survival as the greatest good because that is the boy's task. Men must consider others as well as themselves, or they will end up fighting out of greed, revenge, or the desire to gain advantage. Such a man is not a warrior, but an assassin at work. It is the killer boy who lives by fear, never knowing the greater power of love. Whether he is an inner city gang member, Ku Klux Klansman, or the driver who swerves into another's lane to show his anger, it is the killer boy at work.

King Saul's son Jonathan was as delightful an example of the warrior as we will ever see. He protected his friends and served his God more than family loyalty or ambition. He never fought to prove his power, yet, when he had God to guide him, he would take on an entire army with just his armor bearer for support.

The Apostle Paul tells us that we who serve the Mighty Warrior must ourselves fight, not against flesh and blood, but against the evil of the age we live in and the dark impostor who would destroy lives and mock our King.

Man as King

Every man, enslaved or free, poor or rich, has his area of dominion. Wisdom literature is full of instructions for kings. According to the ancients, the prospect of a fool becoming a king is too horrible to describe. Much of our dominion is shared with others. The more exclusive our dominion and the higher we rise in power, the more our kingdom reflects our style, values, and investment. If earlier generations erred in asserting their dominion too rigidly, this generation has forgotten what is means to be king and to see that justice and truth prevail in their domain.

David, who was every inch a king said, "I will sing of your love and justice... I will walk in my house with blameless heart... No one who practices deceit will dwell in my house; no one who speaks falsely will stand in my presence" (Ps 101:1,2,7). Even if one's kingdom is no bigger than one's own home, the king is to rule it. That means he makes sure that the values worth dying for can live in his kingdom.

This is quite different than what a boy king would seek. The boy king would focus his rule in order to get his own way. What terrible and oppressive domination! Only a real man can be king. A man king seeks values greater than his own life and provides for others as well as himself. He protects and cares for widows, orphans, and the poor.

A man may have dominion alone until he marries. After that, he shares it with his wife and later his children. Sharing dominion is clearly a man-sized task. No boy could consider all the needs involved in such a position of authority. The man who has never been a boy is even more lost, for he does not even know how to take care of himself adequately.

Being a king demands a certain style, for to rule well is to express the deeper values inside. The passion of a poet and the wisdom of the sage are fitting in a king and very satisfying.

Man as Husband

While it may not be for all men, the call to be a husband is the most intense human expression of the task of being a man. A man is to consider the needs of others as equal to his own. Nowhere is that task to be practiced more passionately than in marriage, where the two become one. Not only must the man consider the needs, satisfaction, and feelings of another person, but also he must face a woman who is not like him and often hard for him to figure out. He must also meet her needs at a very intimate level and in almost every aspect of life as he would his own. This is no small challenge. We shudder to think of the disaster if a boy attempts to do such a thing. Go one step further and imagine the disaster of an infant boy getting married who does not even understand his own needs. *Kyrie Eleison!* Lord, have mercy!

Man as Servant

The servant is the expression of a deep and satisfying understanding of the needs of others. Like the wise virgins of the Apocalypse, servants have covered their own needs and are ready to attend to others. In Christian hierarchies, the more people you rule over, the more people you must serve. The boy cannot serve in this way for he will mistakenly conclude that serving makes him the lesser - not as important as the one being served. Like Mother Teresa of Calcutta, the distinguished servant is known by his or her understanding of the master's needs and wishes. The style of service has been perfected by long hours of practice so that the complex now appears effortless. The servant's pride is in his intimate knowledge of the master's needs, which ensures that preparations have been made before the request comes.

Jesus had such style in serving others. Even under the duress of knowing he would be tortured to death within hours, he could say, "In my Father's house are many mansions. I go to prepare a place for you." Now that is room service with style!

Putting it Together

Man is man in all these aspects of his identity. Each title allows a man to express another aspect of who he is and what he can be. One man may fit one title better or feel out of place in another. With the exception of husband, all these titles should be experienced by all men as they grow older. Each one is a dance a man can learn, a tune he can sing, a job he can do, a further expression of the life within him.

The different aspects of a man's identity even blend together at times. They harmonize well with women and children. Understanding his identity in each occasion satisfies a man and gives him a sense of style.

Man is now ready for his next stage—father.

IV. A Father

7. Becoming a Father

It is a mystical moment when the average man learns he is to become a father. He discovers he is now the source of new life. For those who recognize and seize the moment, the universe temporarily disappears and then returns with a penetrating brilliance. Not only history is inexorably changed, but the whole world. Who knows what this new life will bring? The starting gun has sounded, beginning the great race for which he has trained all his life.

As an infant he learned to express his feelings and meet his own needs. Then his father introduced him to the wide world of satisfaction and exertion. In twelve short years, he became a master at knowing himself. He faced the challenge of leaving behind the identity he had just mastered for a new one. At the same time he had learned about his history and how he was to be a part of the future. He had become a man. Shakily at first, but then with rising strength, he learned to meet others' needs along with his own. Fairness and hard bargains became the rule. He now knew how to protect and serve. No sooner had he mastered this identity when once again something deep and frightening, yet good, began to make him uncomfortable. The desire to give life challenged him more than he had ever known. He wanted to become a father.

All his life the mystery of the father pulled at his heart. It was a call beyond bargaining and fairness. It meant giving without being repaid, even suffering for things one didn't do or didn't deserve. To do all this with a sense of fulfillment is the secret joy of being a father. He now wanted it for himself.

Childbirth in this culture increasingly ties fathers to Lamaze classes and the community of women, with fewer ties to the fellowship of men. Becoming a father is nevertheless a male event, participated in only by men, yet never in the absence of women. Becoming a father is often wrongly viewed as what ties a man and woman together, rather than what ties a father and child together.

There is a general undercurrent of belief in society that men are not drawn to fatherhood as strongly as women feel the call to motherhood. Some people feel that women want to get married and have children, but men like to roam and have sex. Yet it is my contention that any man who does not become a father in some meaningful way is doomed to a life of unfulfilled misery. He is like an airplane that never flew, a ship that never sailed, a racehorse that stayed in the stable, an aborted birth. Imagine building a house for twenty years and then not moving into it or preparing twenty-five years for the Olympics and then not competing. Such is the fate of the man who fails to become a father.

To be a father is to give without receiving in return. All men have within themselves the need to be the source of life to others and to give without seeking to receive. This costs personal commitment and expense. To see new life grow takes a lifetime. Anything less and a father is diminished.

Without something to give, a father is like a eunuch on a honeymoon. It is in the strain and effort, and even the failures in fathering, that the best parts of a man are revealed, tested, and strengthened. For this reason, the father welcomes the suffering and cost to himself.

Why does the athlete compete? Why does the actor anxiously wait for the curtain to go up? Why is the Indy 500 driver eager for the green flag? Why does the salesman gear up for a big presentation? Why does the mountain climber seek Mt. Everest? Because it will bring out the best in him. Deep within each of us is the burning desire to put our best on display—tested, tried, demonstrated, and tangible. It is the desire to be known mingled with the call to glory. Being a father brings out what is best in a man.

The torment contestants endure shows us their best. Race drivers crash, burn, break bones, and come back from the hospital to drive again. Football players go on the field with broken bones. Mountain climbers lose their fingers and toes to frostbite. Gymnasts and skaters give up social lives and endure years of grueling practice. All these contestants in the games of life endure hardship so that they can discover and display what is best about themselves. That is what brings satisfaction.

A boy trains to meet his needs. The man trains to meet his needs as well as those of others. This prepares him to have a strong self—to be a person in history, full of life. He is now ready to run the good race, fight the good fight, dance the great dance. He is ready to give life. Only in giving life will he find the deepest, most satisfying expression of what is best about himself. To do so earns him the title of *Father*.

Life is a mystery. To see life spring up where there was none before compels us to look at leaves in the spring or follow Jesus to Lazarus' tomb. It is the most godlike feeling a man can experience without sinning when he can bring life into being. It is the very best part of him.

Stories of Fathers

My friend Rick helped me see how this worked. He had a twelve-year-old daughter when he and his wife conceived again. Together we all shared the excitement for about three months. Then the baby died. As far as the doctors were concerned, Rick's wife had miscarried, but to Rick, his baby had died. He mourned for over a year. To this day he gets tears in his eyes when I ask him about it. One morning over breakfast he said to me, "You know, my feelings about my baby are a little bit selfish. Part of what hurt so much is that being a father brings out the best in me. These are the deepest, strongest feelings I know. And then, to have it all torn away..."

Rick's father had not known the deep satisfaction and joy Rick knew. As he grew up, Rick's dad had told him, "Don't be like me." In fact, he seemed to think that the best thing he could do for Rick was to leave his son alone and let as little as possible of himself rub off on the boy. Rick's father believed that being a father only showed up the worst things about himself.

Travis, my cousin, was looking for a safe and normal life when he had an experience similar to Rick's. One terrible morning he and his wife woke up to find their only child had died of crib death. As we sat by the window looking out at the San Gabriel Mountains, he told me, "When that happened, it changed my life forever." Travis changed careers, lifestyle, and even who he was. Later, as I watched him hug a young bereaved mother, I could see the best in him still looking for a way to be expressed.

Mark has a similar story. His son Jonathan had Down Syndrome and after a short life died from medical complications. Mark was inconsolable with pain. Some of the best of him was cut down in its prime. Mark was a teacher. He knew that Jonathan would need the best of his teaching abilities to make it in the world. He would have to fit into a world that thought he was different and would never fully accept him no matter what he did. Mark took all that he treasured and poured it into his son. When Jonathan died, some of the deepest and best parts of Mark died too.

Mark found the best part of himself as a father, Travis found his deepest understanding, and Rick felt his potential to love. Rick had something to give and knew that fatherhood would bring it into full blossom. He was ready to run the race he had trained for his whole life. Even those bleak days with his own father had helped him see the importance of what a father needed to give.

The truth of the matter goes beyond one's lifetime, however, because fatherhood is an eternal business. Unlike the marriage bond, which is temporal and endures on a good run until "death do us part," paternity is an eternal arrangement.

The parent-and-child relationship is still valid in heaven; otherwise, the promise to Abraham that he will be the father of many nations is a meaningless gesture. Jesus tells us that after Lazarus died, Father Abraham comforted him. What endures eternally is the life-giving family line, not the biological family. Entrance into eternal life is predicated on receiving and giving life.

The Cost of Fatherhood

These eternal bonds between father and child are neither easy nor cheap. For just those reasons they are all the more meaningful to the man who possesses them with understanding. In some ways, they cost the father his very life, whether he measures that in time, energy, or resources. The cost of giving without receiving in return is a kind of dying. With each sacrifice, the father must die a bit and rejoice that he was worthy of glory.

Paradoxically, becoming a father is a process of dying. The new father must leave behind his old understanding of who he is if he is to participate in something new. Most dads do this joyfully, yet with apprehension and fear.

The first cost of fatherhood is to relinquish possessive enjoyment of his wife. If he has been blessed, his wife has been his garden of delights and he—her lover—the object of her devoted love. Yet, when she becomes pregnant, her body, mind, and feelings turn to another, a beloved stranger. This stranger can keep her awake nights when such attempts by her husband would meet with an angry rebuke. He becomes an escort and support, almost an understudy in his wife's heart. There is little that is his alone anymore. He must begin to learn again that having to share his wife does not diminish intimacy.

The newborn emerges from the very privacy which once the father called his exclusive domain. The child, once emerged, lays claim to his wife's breasts and takes over without a care in the world about the father's feelings. For the father who was first a boy and then a man, even this disregard will bring joy, for he knows how much better it is to give than to receive.

It is the cost that lets us know that someone loves us. When someone is willing to suffer for us, then we pay attention. The gift of being a father is to give without receiving in return, to suffer on behalf of someone else. In doing this, the father makes God the Father's love understandable to his own children. He does so not in contrast to the mother, but in concert with her.

Being a father is a man's greatest expression of himself. He is pushed beyond his limits. When men are stretched to new heights, they need encouragement. Formerly all a man needed to say was, "We are expecting a child," and friends and colleagues would pump his hand and congratulate him. Now when a man announces that his wife is pregnant, people say, "Did you want it?" or, "Can you afford it?" or, "Are you going to keep it?" Having babies costs a lot. Raising children is expensive. Dad is supposed to pay the bill, although Mom shares the load too. What is lacking is the encouragement and joy needed to help a man be all that he can be.

The father longs for the opportunity to demonstrate his love. He is eager to fight the good fight because it shows the best of who he is. As his child grows, his opportunities increase and he has to provide even more. Each level of his child's development brings out more of the best of him. He becomes more than he ever thought he could become because of his children. They find in him more than he ever knew he had. Sons and daughters each bring out different aspects of the best of him.

Yet realistically, under the strain of growing, not everything that comes out of fathers is wonderful and life-giving. Growing and stretching also means exposing hidden inadequacies. When a man comes to the time when he is called on to produce the best part of himself and often finds that it is crippled or disfigured, his response can be rage, shame, and distance.

He feels disqualified for the race for which he trained all his life. That can be devastating. His fear of being disqualified may even keep him from entering the race altogether. The good news is he can find healing for the wounded boy inside himself if he will persevere and face the pain.

Let's now explore the relationship between a father and his children.

8. FATHERS AND THEIR CHILDREN

...The essential attribute of the macho— power almost always reveals itself as a capacity for wounding, humiliating, annihilating... He is power isolated in its own potency, without relationship or compromise with the outside world. He is pure incommunication, a solitude that devours itself and everything it touches... He comes from far away: he is always far away. He is the Stranger.

Octavio Paz, *The Labyrinth of Solitude*,
(New York: Grove Press, 1961) 82.

In his classical statement of the male worldview, Octavio Paz has provided a definition of masculinity in his Latin culture. Men exist in a labyrinth of solitude. "We are alone," he says, "solitude, the source of anxiety, begins on the day we are deprived of maternal protection and fall into a strange and hostile world" (82). So men resort instead to "the pistol, a phallic symbol that discharges death rather than life..." (82).

Man is seen as death-giving, father is death-giving, even his humor is death-giving, bringing unexpected annihilation, dust, and nothingness. Power is measured by the ability to destroy and consume. Little wonder that the child deprived of maternal protection is plunged into anxiety, if this is the nature of the father. Millions of people hold this view of fathers or variations on it.

Contrasting with this view of the father as indifferent or even hostile to his children is the image of the father described by the Old Testament prophet Zephaniah (see Zeph 3:17). He is a father who is among his children, like a warrior keeping them safe, singing songs over them, quieting each one with his love, and exulting over them with shouts of joy. This father is no stranger. Instead, he is pure communication. He gives life, not death.

Exploring the Father Bond

But which of these views is the truth about fathers? Which is more realistic? Which behavior can we expect from a father? It is not unusual for psychologists and therapists to argue against the view that fathers are by nature deeply bonded to their children. Therapists might not go as far as Paz with his definition of the masculine soul, but they often seem to believe that men have to "get in touch with their feminine side" in order to bond with their children and develop a nurturing role. There is a widespread view that men who do not embrace their feminine side and, in addition, reject masculine proclivities should never be allowed around children. In this view, held unconsciously by many professionals, men are pure isolation with a sex and power drive thrown in. Being exposed to this sort of "masculine" influence is precisely the fear that torments the children "deprived of maternal protection" in the isolated world Paz describes.

If this destructive nature is not true masculinity but the rage of men with broken bonds, then men who do bond well in the masculine way will resemble Zephaniah's description of a father's love. If you cause a man pain for a long time, especially where it hurts the most, he may become hostile toward everyone. A man separated from his deepest source of satisfaction, meaning, and love may become destructive to himself and others. On the other hand, bonded men will be less hostile, destructive, and angry.

Rick is at home with Ryan. When he drops Ryan off at the play area at the fitness center, Ryan often clings to him for a little while. This behavior mystifies the women that run the center. Why would this little boy cling to his father? Rick says that it was worth having his business go bad to have this time with his son. No one has ever seen him be violent or abusive.

Bob, whose father is also his grandfather, came home to find his wife in bed with his boss. He did not try to kill the other man. Bob is not affluent and his health is not great, but his loyalty to his children makes it hard for him to leave his family without finding a way to care for them.

If it were only an academic issue, it would not matter what a father's bond is toward his children. But it is my contention that this bond is the main event for all males. Without it men are doomed to unhappiness. I believe that fatherhood and motherhood are more the point of our life than religion. God did not tell the couple in the garden to meditate on his words, sing worshipfully, or play the harp, but rather to multiply and fill the earth—dad-and-mom stuff.

This father bond is different with each child. Yet they are more alike than they are different, whether they be sons and daughters or first and last children. Men may even bond more readily than women.

The existence of so many men in the macho category suggests they are more prone to bonding than they appear to be. If so much effort is exerted to prevent bonding, and if men insulate themselves from pain so strongly, perhaps men are hiding a point of great vulnerability and pain. Only someone with a tendency to bond would have to work so hard to prevent it.

In any conflict, the combatants seek to cover up their areas of vulnerability. If men are most vulnerable in the area of their bonds—primarily their bonds to their children—then men who wish to avoid that kind of pain must find ways to stay disconnected from them. They clutter up or even destroy the bonding surface so nothing will stick.

A father will likely stay bonded with his children until the age they reach the highest level of his own growth. Once the child reaches the stage of the father's defeat, Dad must confront his personal crisis again, but now successfully, in order to keep the bond with the child intact and healthy. If he turns away, Dad is faced with the choice of letting his pain cause him to withdraw from the child and break the bond, or else he must cripple his child to ensure that he and the child do not go farther in their growth. It is the strength of this parental bond that has caused many fathers to go through the pain of recovery. Often this bond with their children is the only bond strong enough to keep these wounded fathers from running away.

Take, for instance, Joe. He was the perfect father until Joey was old enough to sleep in his own bed. Joe was patient and enjoyed helping his son, even when Joey couldn't succeed. When Joey was scared at nights and wanted comfort, Joe got him out of his crib and brought him to bed. But one day Joey turned three. By that time he slept in his own bed, wandering only into his parents' room at night whenever he felt the need. Joe found himself telling Joey sharply that since he was now three he needed to stay in his own bed all night.

The first bad night that brought Joey wandering into his parent's bedroom after that produced surprising anger and frustration in Joe. His wife said, "What's gotten into you? You never used to be so harsh. Now you scared him." Joe was surprised at himself, but he said, "He has to learn to stay in his own bed."

A review of his history revealed that Joe's father had become sick at the same time that Joe's younger brother was born, just after Joe himself turned three. What had been a pleasant childhood became rather unforgiving, as irritable parents tried to cope with tough times. Now Joe had to heal and correct his own distortions about being three. Without his son's tears, Joe would have run from his pain and played "hardball" with his son. Joe decided instead to face the truth about his parents' limitations and his own pain. Then he was able to discover, along with Joey, what a three-year-old boy really wants and needs in the middle of the night.

This sort of father is best described as an over-comer. He is motivated by love for his children to face the pain of his own developmental deficiencies and stay bonded to them as they continue to grow.

Much more common is the man who will not bond because he fears the pain. The beliefs about men and pain begin to take their toll as fathers are forced to decide whether life is about avoiding pain or facing it. The man who fails to see the value of pain can best avoid it by keeping his bonding surfaces cluttered with what I call junk bonds. He can love his car, his sports on TV, his fishing or golf, his booze, his work, his religion, or his neighbor's wife. But he neglects his own wife and children, as well as other significant relationships.

Men who believe that they are not the bonding type will not even try to be close to their wife or children. Their lives are cluttered with the junk bonds related to gangs, organized crime, military, and paramilitary groups, hate organizations, travel, and even law enforcement. Musicians have no shortage of music about the non-bonding man who thinks of no one but himself. He is often viewed as a type of man rather than the aberration he truly is.

A man who believes that he must become feminized in order to bond with his children will be greatly frustrated in his attempt to be more like a woman. Women compound this problem by supporting the idea that a good father should bond with a child in exactly the same way as a mother does, and so provide a "back up" for Mom when she is too tired, overwhelmed, or busy. When neither of the parents has ever seen a functional father in action, anyone's guess goes about what a father should be like.

The road to fatherhood is not found through well meaning advice but through seeking satisfaction. For fathers, satisfaction is found by bringing out the best in themselves and giving without receiving in return. This search allows input from the man himself, his wife, children, friends, relatives, and even his children's friends.

Men who believe that bonding should be painless will seek to change and control everyone they bond with to insure that they do not experience pain, anxiety, or loss in their relationships. These bonds can be strong, but they are based on fear and serve to insure that the child never outgrows the parent emotionally. Perhaps this is the most common sort of father. He bonds sufficiently to maintain control but avoids the painful parts of his life where change is needed, unless his wife leaves him or his children provoke him to it. Mostly he tries to keep everyone in order without ever asking himself if keeping it that way satisfies him or anyone.

At each stage of the child's growth the father's own development will affect his fathering differently. Let us see what it is like to be a father as our children grow up.

The Healthy Father and the Infant

New fathers enter what Ken Canfield of the National Center for Fathering calls the age of idealism when their children are first born. Most parents are able to freely join in with their children at this point. Such a bond produces joy and delight between the father and child. Naturally, the father who did not bond with his parents even at this point in his own development will be very poor at parenting himself. He will lack an internal understanding of how things work at this stage and suffer severe levels of emotional pain.

During the first four years of a child's life, the growth and rate of change is enormous. The good dad delights in this growth by observing it carefully and encouraging each new step.

Dad wants to know what his baby can do. Being together is the key to success. The more time spent together, the greater the discoveries. Since this stage of life is usually exhausting for the mother with late night feedings, time spent with Dad is a welcome respite for her. It allows both parents to revel in the life they are building together. This is a new form of intimacy for parents who are not used to being that close when a third person is involved. Mom, Dad, and baby are learning what it means to be a family.

For the father, getting to know his child is a form of rediscovering the world and himself. It is a chance to enrich his sense of the world. In revisiting a child's world, the father will experience a feeling much like falling in love with his son or daughter. This rush of experience and feeling occurs as everything becomes new and live again. It is tempered by the exhaustion that most parent's experience in the early years of child rearing in a culture that tends to isolate parents from other support.

The father who was raised in relative isolation and never participated in raising children must overcome his early years spent alone and his limited sense of self. Repulsion with diapers, fear of holding babies, and reluctance to coo and snuggle must be overcome to form a close relationship with his newborn. This is all part of the discovery of himself and the world that the first-time father experiences. This prepares him to appreciate his later children for who they are, so he can meet their needs more accurately even if he has less time available per child.

The Wounded Father and the Infant

The father whose own development was arrested at the infant stage is faced with a monumental task in raising children. When relating with his children, he will either prove to be neglectful and distant or controllingly overprotective. This overprotectiveness is the source of emotional and physical abuse. A father who was sexually abused at this stage will typically experience his desire to bond with his child, whether male or female, as a sexual impulse. Closeness of any kind in his experience involves sexual activity and may result in repeating the abuse or rigidly removing himself from his children in angry isolation.

While it is unlikely that any severe abuse at this age will be corrected without a great amount of pain and healing, most fathers discover only mild deficits that require them to overcome their discomfort, anxiety, and embarrassment at entering the baby's world. The father who knows what satisfies him will excitedly plunge through this barrier and may soon be changing diapers, giving baths, and taking baby on walks—all with a "daddy" feel to it. In addition, he will rediscover the world with his child, feeling the joy of encountering a whole new world once again.

Wilbur was one father who did not make it through his infant years intact. In fact, while his parents neither abused nor neglected him in any criminal way, they treated him in the same way one might treat a prize-winning cow. He received his food regularly, his stall was clean, his pasture fenced, and he got his shots on time. His father and mother worked hard but never stopped to find him interesting. As a result, it never occurred to him that he or, later, his six children were the least bit interesting. This might seem odd in a man with a doctorate in counseling.

Each child received his or her food regularly, each was always squeaky clean, and each one got his or her shots on time. He never thought to notice the gifts his children brought him or to compliment them on what they made in school. He didn't think to play with their toes or fingers, or blow on their tummies. When they grew up and got married, he never thought to ask their boyfriends or girlfriends what they liked, believed, or even where they wanted to live.

At his retirement party, many students from his school claimed he had been a guiding influence on them—after all it was his job and he worked hard—but his own children did not all attend. Some even declared they had no tribute to give. Wilbur didn't seem to notice. He didn't see why his children should be interested in him, anyway. He expressed no need or feeling and sought no satisfaction from his children. He simply cared for them with the dispassionate interest that seemed right because that's how he had been raised.

Due to the interest shown by some family friends, some of Wilbur's children began to express their needs and feelings. Soon the family began to disintegrate, although Wilbur never thought to look at himself to see if he were part of the problem because he found himself totally uninteresting. The real problem was that Wilbur got lost as an infant. He had no sense of being loved for who he was, no sense of being someone special.

The Healthy Father and the Child

As the child nears four years of age, the father begins to find himself increasingly teaching the child. It is the time to answer incessant "why" questions and explain everything about the world. The father who has explored the world with his child for the last several years will find these questions excite his own curiosity and add zest to life. Teaching and learning go together.

It is a time of imagination as much as a time for facts, because the child finds it easier to imagine the impossible than to understand the actual. Fantasies of being big and living in Daddy's world have special meaning. Little boys want to be like Dad and marry Mom, while little girls want to marry Dad and take better care of him than Mommy does.

This is also a time for fears to grow. As the transformation into childhood approaches, the child discovers that others— usually siblings—increasingly compete for his or her coveted spot. Jealous rage, possessiveness, and a desire for exclusive relationships with one's parents characterize this age.

The healthy father takes time to teach his children about inclusive love by teaching his children how to take care of themselves, pets, toys, and younger children. This is at the level of caring play and not adult responsibilities. It is sharing toys and Daddy's knee and helping little sister or brother stay on Daddy's back for a ride.

The healthy father approaches weaning his child with anticipation. Once weaned, children are able to explore the world with Dad much more freely. After the initial apprehension subsides, the child is free to pass from imagination to learning. Very soon school will begin and with it the need to understand the outside world of strangers. School is like a giant bicycle for the child to ride and master.

Fathers help their children learn to use comparisons, rules, and competition to measure their own growth, not their own value. One key area of learning at this age involves the conscience of each child. Within a warm and strong relationship with parents, rules, and examples are carefully matched to see if the rule maker follows the rule.

Dad is the one who keeps the secret knowledge of the good things inside each of his children. With patience born of faith, he searches diligently until the good part of his child is discovered, or a lesson is learned. At these times the child learns to be more than he or she was before, simply because not everything we discover was there before we began the search.

It is soon apparent that Dad and Mom are not the only teachers that their child will need. They are key to the child's need to know the meaning of what they learn, particularly through comparisons. It is easy for people to see what they are not. Becoming what one has not yet become is much harder to believe.

My older son Jamie told me once that he didn't think he could ever be the kind of father that I am. It is impossible for a teenager to imagine himself raising children as well as years of diligent effort have taught me to do. What I know that he doesn't is the difference between what he now knows at seventeen and what I knew when I was his age. I have every hope and expectation that he will surpass me as a father in twenty-four years.

The Wounded Father and the Child

The father who remained stuck at the child stage in his own life will not know how to guide his children through their sense of jealousy and fear. He will already have struggled with jealousy over the bond between his wife and child. This may lead to weaning the child too early as well as increased fear and jealousy in the child. Often such a father has isolated his wife from her friends, so she is more vulnerable to exhaustion and discouragement and more dependent on him. Yet he is unable to support her without anger.

In response to this crisis, the wounded father will often angrily or coldly reject his sons and foster his daughter's immature, jealous attachment to himself. In doing so he seeks to keep for himself alone what his children can give, rather than teaching them what they have to offer others. For his daughter this often means she must stay Daddy's girlfriend forever. The son becomes a slave who can only compete for Mother's attention when Dad is away. This may prove a training ground for the son to have mistresses later on.

Tom was a father whose life had fallen apart during his childhood stage. His parents took to fighting and his dad left. As time went on, he began to call his dad by his first name and treat him just like his step-dad. In reality Tom had no dad. Since, like all children at this age, you are what you learn, he learned to be his own dad. He went on to one school after another, he got degrees in religion, business, and education.

Tom married young and had three children who did well until they reached school age. From then on, Tom's anger grew. He angrily compared his children with each other, and with others outside the family. He compared them with the rules he had set and found them all wanting. Tom compared his wife with the other women who were smarter, thinner, more pleasing, less passive, better dressed, had bigger thises and smaller thats and were better with money. His family began to like it when he went away on business because they were tired of being yelled at and feeling angry or afraid.

Tom could not see why they simply didn't learn to be what he told them to be, what the Bible told them to be, what good psychological theory told them to be, what any intelligent person could see they should be. Had Tom ever stopped to ask he might have noticed that he was not satisfied with life, but rather than seek satisfaction he made rules and berated his family. They, in turn, learned to feel bad, sneak around his rules, counter with rules of their own, and likewise be dissatisfied. If it wouldn't make them feel so bad, they might have even wished him dead.

Meanwhile, Tom regularly became dissatisfied with his church, his friends, his job, his house, and the part of the country he lived in. He decided that he would move to a new location, dragging his unhappy family along with him. In this, he had at least improved on his own father, for he did take his children out to see the world without abandoning them. He only made them wish at times that he would.

Tom simply could not see why his family did not learn to become the people he wanted them to be. He didn't know that while it is important to produce products with your efforts, that principle works for things but not for people. A father's hope became despair for Tom, because he could only see in his family what they were not.

Healthy Father to Young Men and Women

Contrary to popular belief, I do not think that there is much difference between a father's relationship to his daughters and his sons. The primary difference involves the way in which a father affirms his children's sexual identity. For the son the message is, "Your sexuality is like mine and that is very fine." For the daughter the message is, "Your sexuality is the opposite of mine and that is very fine." For both sexes of children, the major factor is the father's respect for his own sexuality and lack of fear of theirs.

The father of young men and women enjoys the onset and development of true friendship with his children. Having reached the crucial goals of development together, the father must first allow the independence of his children, followed by their return and a review of their progress. Once again life is like a dance with the endless rhythm of goings and comings. The first of these movements away from Dad is likely to be painful because the young adult must find his or her own group identity separate from Mom and Dad. The first step is often to declare oneself different than one's parents on some important point. To some parents this appears to be rejection. Daughters want to be women and have their own boyfriends. Sons want to be different in ways that often mean ignoring Dad for a few years in favor of their own friends and interests. If Dad is prone to fear rejection, he will use these cues to withdraw from his children rather than encouraging their development.

As adult children approach different milestones, they turn to their father for encouragement, then run off and forget him only to return later for his praise, interest, and appreciation of their success. Should, per adventure, their efforts result in failure, their return is likely to be quicker. When faced with his children's failures, Dad gets a chance to relive a little of the "kiss the boo-boo" days before the cycle repeats. Major milestones are first dates, driving the car, getting a job, going to college, getting engaged and then married, buying a car or a house, or even new tires.

I can recall trying to decide whether I should buy steel-belted or radial ply tires and asking my dad to help me choose. The same was true as to what car battery was best or what sort of life insurance policy I needed. These sorts of decisions brought me back to Dad long after I was married.

The character of a father-and-child relationship in adulthood becomes increasingly like that of adult peers. As children begin to approach the same point in life at which they can actually remember watching their parents, times of sharing take on a special sweetness. "I remember thinking how old my parents were at thirty-five and now I'm thirty-five." Adult children are now eager to compare their experiences with what they remember of their parents as well as what they experience. How am I different? How am I like my parents? For parents this fulfills the old prophecy, "You'll understand when you're older," and, provided that they let their children make the point, it now cements the bond.

A father is gratified with each renewal of his children's interest in who he is. Each incident allows him renewed opportunity to express how much of his children he has treasured and guarded inside, and how he has blended all the forces that made the child unique.

The Wounded Father of Young Men and Women

The father who crashed as he attempted passage into manhood is in for a bumpy ride when his children take the steering wheel. He will find strong impulses to react the way his parents did or precisely the opposite. Since the most common symptom of this problem is a continuation of the reactive identity of early teenage years, this father is usually marked by being reactive and negative towards his children. He may criticize the way his children dress, their choice of friends, their personal styles, or their approach to college and work.

A reactive identity is one where the person defines him- or herself in terms of what he or she is not. It can range from the response, "I'm not stupid, you are," to the complex, "I'm not like my parents and family." It is seen in tastes and choices. Reactive identities know what they don't like or want or value, but not what they do like, want, and value.

The second error common to fathers who experienced trouble during their own coming of age is that they tend towards extremes—that is to say their own style is reactive. They are either too involved and controlling or too withdrawn and detached. They provoke standoffs and draw lines in the sand, making every move their child makes a challenge to Dad's authority. Even steps towards normal growth become major risks for the child because Dad says, "If you move out, don't expect any help from me!"

Most fathers who are caught in this trap can't believe it is more about them than about their children. They are trying so hard and really believe they are doing the right thing. Never do they stop to ask if they are satisfied, rather they concern themselves with being justified. They typically react against their wife's observations and the feelings of their other children with more self-justification. Since they have not become men, they do not seek the correction of other men either, although if they did they might soon grow up and turn their hearts towards their children.

In most cases it is the strength of the father's bond with his children that inspires him to provide for his children the very things he did not receive. He feels with them the emotions he was not allowed to experience. In giving this life to his children, the father finds expression for the very best part of himself. This bond is both his connection to the world and his incentive to make the world better.

9. THE FATHER'S WORLD

If indeed it is good to be a man, then how rewarding it is to be a father! The father is a source of life to others. Every man who does not become a source of life to others will remain unfulfilled, even miserable. The man who lives to be a consumer with the most toys will die. He must still give up his life, but only when he can no longer enjoy it.

The man who gives life only to insure his own supply of pleasure is shocking to us. This is the kind of person who inspires children's stories of witches who fatten children up so they can eat them. The most common version of this horror is the man who acts fatherly and then sexually abuses the children he lures into his grasp. When fathers do this to their children or stepchildren, we call it incest. When men fatten up other people's children to eat, we call it pedophilia. Whatever name we use, the revulsion and horror remain because life-giving is not intended as a way to insure the life-giver's supply of pleasure.

What about the case where the child is not the biological relative of the man? The story of the good Samaritan teaches that a neighbor is defined by acting neighborly to everyone he or she meets. Likewise, any man entrusted with the care of children is a father to them. He will be judged accordingly. The privilege of giving life prohibits consuming for our own pleasure the life we give. To the one who has been given much, much will be required.

Man's basic nature is fatherly, yet actual examples of fatherliness are rare.

Seldom is there a fair distribution of resources. We often see a few fathers doing the *yeoman's share*, while other potential fathers do nothing and suffer pangs of emptiness. A man who has no biological child often feels most acutely the calling of fatherhood. For emotional or economic reasons, he may have decided not to have a child in order to protect that child from facing a cruel world. As a father to a phantom child, he feels the empty yearning of protecting without the joy of giving life.

Many couples are childless for other reasons. Rather than list possible reasons, we will focus on the need for everyone to experience giving life. Even the single man whom we will study in the next chapter must give life to those who need a supplementary, stand-in, or replacement father. In this way, he will help balance the load for other fathers and find fulfillment for himself.

Every child, even in the best of homes, needs supplementary fathers. These are fathers who assist the child's main father with training, introducing the child into the community as well as appreciating parts of the child and the world that the father does not know. Supplemental fathers are needed not only in childhood, but throughout life.

Sometimes, due to illness, death, distance, moral breakdown, or abandonment, a primary father does not provide even the minimum requirements for his children. These children require a partial replacement of their father. This stand-in father will take the father's place at significant moments in the child's life. One young woman wanted her favorite uncle to give her away at her wedding after the death of her father. A young man wanted someone to watch him compete in sports after his father left town with another woman. This role is like that of a foster father or godfather.

Faced with a catastrophic loss of a parent through violence, crime, moral delinquency, or disaster, some people face the need for a new father or mother. Legal adoption is needed for children and its spiritual equivalent for adults. Since almost all my close friends have adopted children, I have observed many replacement fathers.

There are many different levels at which it is possible to be a father. Since there is a great demand for good fathers, men are never at a loss for opportunities. No one with only one father has enough fathers.

Man as Father to His Wife

Every man will marry a woman who has deficits in her bonds with her father. Every woman will marry a man who has deficits in his bonds with his mother. Healthy couples often address this problem by temporarily serving as supplemental parents for each other. When one partner slips into their childhood feelings, the healthy spouse will respond like a good parent should.

Within a healthy marital bond there is room for both part-
ners to be adults at the same time in order to run a household. In order to play, both can then be children at the same
time. In order to heal and straighten themselves out they can
even occasionally be parent and child to each other. At times,
it is also permissible for the arrangement to be lopsided with
one spouse doing more parenting and the other more feeling,
provided the arrangement is understood to be temporary.

Older couples sometimes find themselves in a parent-child
relationship due to illness, accidents, and calamity. This is a
different situation than it is to enter a marriage in order to
find a parent. Most women who try to marry a father-figure
are still at the four-year-old level of emotional development.
Four-year-old girls want to marry Daddy and are sure they
can take better care of him than Mommy can. However, girls
who have not outgrown this stage by the time they marry
carry within themselves the jealous rage of childhood. A four-
year-old girl wants to be special, the only girl in Daddy's life.
She wants only to protect her place with Dad. Such behavior
is tolerable, even a bit cute, in a four-year-old. But when
lodged in an adult body with its knowledge and abilities, jeal-
ously becomes a terror and a horror.

Four-year-old children and their adult counterparts give
care, based on the hope that in giving they will receive equal
care in return. This version of consuming the life one gives
leads to an endless succession of upsets as hurt rage follows
hurt rage.

The man who joins himself to a woman after mistaking her
devoted love for Daddy with an adult love for a husband will
rue the day he said, "I do." Not only so, but should the
woman outgrow this four-year-old stage at some point, she
will lose interest in taking care of her man, leaving her ex-
husband to feel that she took him in with promises of love
but then took him for everything she could.

The man trapped in such an arrangement often buys security by using his life-giving capacity to insure his own source
of supply. He will often expect to take care of such a woman

in return for having her please him. Since life-giving carries with it the prohibition of consuming the life we give for our own pleasure such arrangements always backfire. Long-term father-and-daughter relationships are an inadequate model for a marriage relationship.

It is often the woman who encourages her husband to become a better father for their children. In doing so, she receives some vicarious fathering herself. Since Father is the prototypical male in every daughter's life, she understands her femininity primarily in relationship to Dad's masculinity. Anything a husband does to change his wife's view of men or her femininity makes him, for that moment, a supplemental father. This is a helpful role and even healing.

A man told me how his wife had hidden one of his shirts that she did not like. When he asked her to return it, she said, "You can beat me if you want, but I won't get it." Raised by an abusive father, she could not appreciate her husband's patience and concern.

"I knew I was speaking for good fathers everywhere," he told me, "when I said, 'I'm not going to hurt you. I just want my shirt.'" Then he gave her a hug. In that moment, he was a supplemental father for his wife. He was a life-giver.

Man as a Father to His Children's Friends

"Enough for us and some to share." This motto should be found in every home. It is a good measure for the amount of love needed to produce satisfaction. Enough for us with some to share is the dosage of attention children need. On open house nights at school, the parents who pay attention to their child's efforts and those of the child's friends or tablemates become popular and spread a blanket of goodwill for the child to enjoy in school. Even in such places as scouts, baseball leagues, or camps, the parents who pay attention to their children's friends really stand out. Not only so, but the parent who sends along an extra cookie for the child to share, or makes room for one more on the way to the amusement park or church, allows their child to share the best treasure — his parents. Comments like, "Your dad is cool!" or, "Your mom is really nice!" please parent and child alike.

If you look around, you will find parents that almost always have an extra participant in family activities. Children in such families are provided the means to give good experiences to friends. They prove that their dad and mom are the greatest.

I once read a true story of a father who allowed his daughter and her little friend to "fix" his hair. He then took them both to a restaurant with his outrageous styling job. This allowed his daughter to share her wonderful dad and approach life with the vision of "enough for us with some to share."

Men as Godfathers

In various sacramental traditions, the role of the godfather is a very special one. In Spanish, the word for godfather is "compadre," or literally "co-father." Besides the spiritual responsibility to bring the children up in the ways of the Lord should the father be absent, co-fathers used to provide real-life security for the children in a world where illness or war could claim the father's life and leave the child unprotected. Thus fathers saw it as one of their first duties before God to obtain a back-up father who would make a commitment to care for each of their children for life.

The idea of a father and co-father agreeing to the mutual care of a child has many spiritual, social, and personal advantages. This role provides a way for single men to participate in fathering. Right from the start it also gives children a sense of a spiritual family which extends beyond biological ties.

Man as a Father After Divorce

Single-Parent Dads

The first and most obvious result of divorce is the presence of two single parents. In addition to the effort of single parenthood, there is a lot of emotional pain which brings out hidden problems and hides other problems.

Carrying this burden, the single parent who is a father must do his best to be both Mom and Dad. Although this is impossible, it must be attempted nevertheless to avoid further polarization of the parents and of gender-specific roles. Children need attention on a daily basis, both to what goes in and what comes out. This leaves single parents to be both father and mother when they have custody of the children. Since the wise father always find other fathers (and, in this case, mothers) for his children, he will need to lean more heavily on their help in order to avoid collapse.

Dad and his Ex-Wife

Some have said that the mother is the main interpreter of the father to her children. Through her eyes, they come to view his time at work as an act of love or a way to stay away from his family. Never is the father more vulnerable to this kind of interpreting than during a divorce and while separated from his children. Wise mothers interpret the father's actions truthfully, not according to their own moods and fears.

The dad who knows himself to be a life-giver will continue to care for his children. He will avoid, as best he can, wasting life and resources in fighting his ex-wife. The major trap for divorcing couples is when both parties react to each other rather than express who they really are. Instead of Dad acting like the man and father he knows himself to be, he allows hurt and trapped feelings to take over. This in turn leads to rejection and avoidance.

The determination to live according to one's own character should rule in relationship to one's ex-wife. The father must do his best to become the faithful interpreter of his own actions—actions which while loving may not be understandable to children. Children, particularly young children, do everything because it is what they want and like to do. Thus, they will interpret all their parents' actions to mean the same. If Dad or Mom is not with them, it is because the parent does not like to be with them. Parents are always viewed as doing what they like.

To avoid making these childish misunderstandings a permanent part of the child's identity, the wise father will give an interpretation of his and his ex-wife's actions that is realistic. These interpretations will need to be made repeatedly until the child is able to understand a world in which people do not always do what they like to do.

The final goal is to give life to children. If they cannot have one home in which they grow up loved and wanted, they now have two homes in which to grow up loved and wanted.

Dad as Stepfather

Divorces tend to happen because people's ability to love is exceeded by the force of their feelings. In other words, people divorce because their feelings change. The most common explanation given to children about divorce is, "Your parents don't love each other any more." This makes for a terrifying situation for children, who can then never be sure when love will run out for them as well. They also learn that one you love is not a matter of choice, but how you feel. This lesson is clearly applied in the relationship to step-fathers. Since Mom did not love Dad, just because he was Dad, neither will the child love Step-dad just because he is Step-dad. Stepparents, therefore, often inherit the storm of feelings that the child now believes are the rule of life. The rule goes something like this: "If I love you, fine, but if I don't, then any treatment or rejection is justified." Most children of divorce are left with an internal rule similar to this. It is the bane of blended families.

Step-fathers may experience a slow progression from being a supplemental father to a replacement father. In other cases, which usually involve younger children, men may find themselves suddenly thrust into the father role with no time for adjustment. Men find it quite painful when their father love is rejected by their new wards. The man who has not learned the value of a love that suffers will withdraw or become controlling and angry. He then ceases to love as a dad and becomes the boss instead.

At the other extreme is the stepfather who, rather than giving life as a father would, consumes it for his pleasure. His attraction to the children is more likely to become sexual since he has not gone through the process of cleaning dirty diapers, getting spit up on, staying up nights, cleaning a filthy face, or even getting a finger up his nose. It is all those irritating moments of closeness that help most fathers develop a nonsexual touch and love for his children.

The man who knows his feelings, his needs, and what will bring him satisfaction will find step-parenting to be a satisfying expression of his ability to give life when he realizes that he has nothing to prove. He is a dad and his job is finding ways to express the best of himself. If his audience appreciates him, that's fine. If they do not, then his character will shine even brighter. He is still a father whether anyone appreciates it or not. Children do not make a father. They only provide the opportunity for a man to express his fatherliness.

The Father and His Work

No chapter on being a father would be complete without mentioning his work. Most dads find their work to be the most continuous part of fatherhood as well as the thing that prevents them from being the dad they want to be. One friend of mine said that a book on being a dad need contain only one page—a picture of a man taking out his billfold. One woman said that the difference between a father's relationship with his daughter and his son is that the son wants the keys to the car and the daughter wants the credit card. Credit card, car keys, and billfold all depend on a man's work. Yet it is work that keeps Dad from the track meet after school, the violin recital, and the class play. Work puts Dad in a bad mood by the time he gets home and drains the best of his energy before he can make good on his promise to play ball in the park.

Unlike Matthew, who "rode on his daddy's shoulders, behind a mule, beneath the sun," in the John Denver song, most American boys and girls do not work with their dads. Some, like the children in *Mary Poppins*, venture into their father's workplace almost in wonder or even fear.

To a man, his work is his life poured out minute by minute and returned to him in an envelope every two weeks. When the government, unions, insurance companies, and other parasites have taken their share, all but the most wretched of men will take what is left of their earnings home to keep their family alive. It might not seem like much, and in spite of all the quips about "bringing home the paycheck," this too is life-giving.

A man who knows he is a good thing and can give away the life he has received will have many opportunities to do so. He must be strong or his life will be stolen before he can give it away. He must know who he is or he will be shaped into whatever pleases the consumers around him. This life-giving ability is the main event in men's lives. In the next chapter we will see how men who have not become fathers biologically express this life.

10.   SINGLE AND CHILDLESS MEN AS FATHERS

Men have something of great value to give to children. They are to be the source of life to others, because God grants them the ability to see other people as they were meant to be. A father is one who helps his children find their true identity in spite of cultural distortions and his own injuries. It is not the getting married or starting a pregnancy that makes a man able to see others with the eyes of God.

It was the prayer of my teenage years that God would let me see Jesus in others. When I looked at a girl and said, "Now, where do I see Jesus in her?" it had an influence on how I treated her. To this day, seeing Jesus in a boy changes my attitude towards him. My teenage prayer was the beginning of a gift. Seeing people as God would see them helped me act accordingly. The driver who gave me the finger and honked his horn became blind and small rather than large and threatening. Girls without bras became lonely and needy instead of being the keepers of the great treasure. I now had a gift to give anyone who would receive it. Seeing into someone's heart is perhaps the greatest gift a man can give. Fathers give this gift when they help others to see themselves correctly.

Julie has very few friends. Her own father never affirmed her. When people said insulting and vulgar things to her she answered in kind. "Everyone hates me," she told her pastor, who was also her replacement father. "Everyone hates me, except for you. You keep telling me that I'm a blessing. Why do you tell me that I'm a blessing?"

"Because that is what God created you to be," said her pastor. "It is a father's job to tell you the truth about yourself.

You were created to be a blessing, and anything other than that is a lie."

Every man was created to be a blessing. It is the only reason God created men, not to be a curse, but a blessing. Even though a father may not have followed God's design, the father within every man is called to be a blessing to his children.

Julie's father had put other things in her heart. Every time she got angry her father would say, "What's-a-matter, you need to get laid?" Little wonder that in time her first reaction when provoked was a two-word phrase ending in "you!"

When we can see the image of God in others, we begin giving them life and form. This desire comes from the father heart in every man. Single men, as well as married men without children, are capable of this type of life-giving. They will be unfulfilled without it.

God established men as protectors and nurturers of his garden. To be a man means to protect and make things grow. This is the basis of fatherhood. If a man's own history has not been redeemed by God, he will have nothing redeemable to offer to others. He cannot see others through the eyes of heaven and so bring them life. If a man can only see garbage in others, he will not know who they were created to be.

Men who have the eyes of heaven and a redeemed history are ready to be fathers, whether to their extended families or spiritual families. The man who offers such gifts to others is being a father whether he is married, has children, or is single.

Certainly a case can be made that to be a spiritual father it is better to remain single and celibate. Marriages demand time, energy, and resources. In I Corinthians 7, Paul says it is better not to marry unless sexual passions are too strong. In order to understand this passage we need to read verse 26, which speaks of "a time of stress like the present," and verse 29, which says, "The time we live in will not last long," referring to a moment in the ongoing life of the church. Paul was writing to a church under violent, horrifying persecution.

Having lived through times of persecution when Christians were driven from their homes in the middle of the night and forced to escape with their wives and children, I find Paul's description to be true. The missions context in which I grew up in Colombia was exceedingly violent at times. When fleeing for his life, a married man is not thinking of the Lord's children. He has to think about his wife and children and how to find them food and shelter. As Paul describes, it is a bad time to marry and raise a family. If one can handle it, staying single does save grief and pain. Those who have seen their children tortured or starved to death will witness the truth of this statement.

During times of extreme stress the single person can and does devote time to the care of others. A single person can be a supplemental stand-in or replacement father, a brother or a friend to more people than a married man can. Pastors and missionaries who plan to go into high-stress locations should listen to Paul's excellent instruction and stay out if they are married with children. In any case, Paul is clear that the single person can care for more children than the married person if he or she is devoted to Christ.

Under normal conditions, marriages do form the most desirable way of having children because they are the most uniform and disciplined way of providing care for a family. The non-stop effort afforded by a lifetime commitment to one's child produces character which cannot be duplicated by any other method. The parent who throughout life sustains a child's life and growth develops a breadth of love that covers all things. The single person who, in times of severe stress, loves many children and endures the deaths of many children builds a depth of love that cannot be duplicated either. Both loves are strong because they flow from the person's life itself—life which in turn flows from God.

The call for single men to become fathers goes far beyond stressful periods in history to stressful times in everyday life. Every child needs more than one father. Many single men do not have the opportunities because they have hidden their desire to become fathers.

If single men do not know having children is satisfying, they will not desire children. Men who look inside themselves will find something pulling them toward children—something pushing them to be a source of life. Some will recognize it for what it is, the call to be a father.

The Infant

There are actually many places for a single man to experience fatherhood. It is hardest for single men to become fathers to infants. Few opportunities are afforded except within the extended family context where they do find opportunities to become father figures. This is the most natural place to experience the long-term commitment of fatherhood. No child with only one father has enough fathers. Naturally, if the child has no father, his or her need will be greater. Nieces, nephews and younger cousins all provide opportunities for the single man to experience fatherhood.

The Child

All fathers are life-givers. The single man should express the life that lies within himself whether it comes out through cooking, hiking, art, music, sports, working, exploring, or simply talking. This is the life he has to offer children. The child is beginning to explore life and seek satisfaction. He needs the life that the single man finds within himself. It is a simple matter to share what one loves with children by simply including them.

If he cannot find such a child within his extended family, the man may seek children within organizations in his community or through his church. As with biological fathers, single men should seek more than one father for their children. An isolated father is always in trouble, and single men should not think they have been granted an exemption to this rule. Parents should be warned not to share their children with fathers or mothers who live and act alone; trouble will usually come of it. By living alone, I do not mean people who live by themselves in their own house or apartment, but those whose practice of parenting is solitary whether they live with others or not.

Becoming a father to children is easy for most single men. Not only are there opportunities like children's clubs, Sunday schools, and group sporting events, but many single men can be fathers in junior high ministries. Junior high is the time that many children experience their first conscious rejection by their fathers. Fathers often react to their children by rejecting their independence at a time when children are still very concerned about their parents' attention. In many churches, camps, and activity centers, this parenting gap is filled by young would-be fathers.

Sports is another arena where single men tend to congregate. Older brothers, single uncles, and occasional sports enthusiasts become supplemental fathers to young players learning the ropes. Most single men stay at the supplemental-father stage. Occasionally, an uncle will become a stand-in father for his nephews and nieces, particularly following a divorce or a father's death.

Young Adults

Single men also have a wonderful opportunity to be fathers when boys go through their rite of passage into manhood. Single men have as much to teach boys about history and manhood as married fathers do. They often have more time, so their contributions can be greater.

Fathers are needed as children become adults. Young men and women often need someone to help them when conflicts escalate at home. A single man can even become a replacement father through adoption or foster parenting. One pastor I know, although he never married, took in a boy and a girl who were abandoned teenagers. These new charges lived with him until they were adults. He paid for the girl's wedding and helped the boy buy a car. He became, in all important respects, their father for life.

Becoming a Good Father

To experience fatherhood fully, the single man must take time to consider what he is doing. Fathers need to take time to think about being fathers. They must ask themselves, "What would a father do in this or that situation?" The single man may think his lack of ideas on how to be a successful father comes from his lack of biological children, but that is not true. Even with biological children, fathers learn to act like fathers by asking themselves, their friends, and family, "What would a father do now?"

Many men find their first answers to the question about what a father would do have something to do with punishment. For many, their conscious thoughts about fathering have never gone beyond spanking, grounding, or shouting. We should encourage each fledgling father or single man to seek the things instead that make him feel he is giving life to children in his care.

In practice there should be no separation of married fathers and single men who father. What is needed by both types of fathers is the strength and experience of their elders, the true *Grand Fathers* of the community. It is grandfathers who help men become fathers—just as fathers help boys become men. And that is our next topic.

V. AN ELDER

11.   BECOMING AN ELDER

The first house I bought belonged to Walter Gilbert, a schoolteacher. At the back of the house was what Walter called a "mother-in-law apartment." There his mother-in-law and after her many other people found shelter. When he retired, Walter took very seriously his status as an elder. He helped his pastor care for many who came to the church for help. Walter took care of others in need. One neighbor, fleeing the Holocaust, bought a plot of land from Walter when he arrived in the United States. To the end of his life he told stories about the kindness and fairness of "Mr. Walter."

Our lives are full of history. We are heirs to rich traditions of elders—their stories quietly lived out around us. Somewhere along the way many of us have forgotten to investigate our roots as our elders quietly pass away. We become a generation that believes that relevance means new data. However, data becomes obsolete. Pages of statistical analysis from my dissertation are no longer relevant today. Yet we madly pursue the new, assuming that old information is no longer important. We too easily forget the treasures found only in the minds of the elders. As a result we disregard the importance of becoming an elder.

We will use "elder" rather than "grandfather" or "mentor" to refer to the final stage of manhood. We define the term as "a man who has raised all his children to be adult men and women and is ready to be a father to others outside his immediate family." Age does not make an elder. It is the readiness to treat others in your community as you have treated your own family that makes a man an elder.

It is understood in many tribal societies that ruling is left to elders. These elders maintain the history and culture of their people. In India men are expected to reach a point in their lives where their concerns expand beyond their own house to include their village. The home is the training ground for the elder, who having practiced on those born to him, can now be trusted with the lives of those whom he did not father. Elders guard, teach, and oversee. In this way they are fathers to their people, the stranger, and the orphan.

Octavio Paz said of the "macho" man, "He is not of our city." The macho man is the antithesis of the elder because he measures his masculinity by death and consumption, not by preserving and giving life. When elders use a macho view of life to protect tradition and their own village, the results are violent and oppressive.

King David, on the other hand, was an elder in a life-giving tradition, although he was a man of war. When his city was raided and all the women, children, and riches were carried off, David went after the raiders with his army to rescue them. The real evidence of his elder capacity came when he returned and insisted that the recovered goods be shared between those who went to battle and those who stayed and stood guard. He looked to the best interests of all the members of his community.

Elders become elders, rather than tyrants, by going through all of the stages of life. You will recall that each stage builds on the previous one rather than replacing it. And elder has gone through the process of becoming a child many times— once with each child he raised, in addition to his own childhood. This equips him with refined and mature knowledge of his needs, feeling, and sources of satisfaction. He will have introduced each child to the community while helping the child explore and understand his or her world. He will have found elders who will act as supplemental fathers for his own children. He will have learned from other fathers how to teach each child his or her place in the family history.

All of the elder's own children will have become men or women—that is to say, they will be over twelve years old. Only then will a man be ready to consider becoming an elder. He will have trained and will be training his children to treat others fairly. This kind of experience will have allowed the man approaching the status of elder to understand the needs and feelings and the required satisfaction of many people within his community. He will also be aware of the dangers his community contains since he has worked for years to protect his children.

The apostle Paul uses many of these characteristics in his description of elders to Timothy and Titus (I Tim 3:1-7; Tit 1:6-9). An elder should have his home, his beliefs, and himself in good order. At home an elder should have one wife and orderly children. His home should overflow with hospitality. His ties to his community will be strong and intact. His reputation will be a good one. The elder's own life should be orderly. He must be a good teacher and a friend to many.

In his doctrine, the elder must know God and God's view of people. He faithfully sees other people through the eyes of heaven. Thus, he is able to exercise a spiritual fatherhood for those in his care.

It is apparent from even a cursory examination of these characteristics that an elder is well at home with his needs and feelings, able to satisfy himself and others, well practiced in fairness, an experienced father, one who gives love, one who suffers without growing angry or resentful. The elder carries within himself the life experience of an infant, a boy, a man, and a father.

There is no shortcut to maturity. Becoming an elder requires a high degree of mastery of each one of the preceding stages. The rewards for elders are great. Elders often receive a double inheritance for their endurance since they father both biological and spiritual children.

The passage into the status of elder often arrives through the marriage of a man's children. Fathers adopt additional children when their own children marry. Fathers who have long taken interest in their children's friends have anticipated the day of adoption eagerly. In giving away their children to others, they receive children in return, and how great that joy can be. Being welcomed into an accepting and loving family is wonderful for brides and grooms. How hurtful it is when the parents are judgmental or rejecting! Fathers and elders know that their love has children as its reward. Weddings celebrate this adoption, which is why last names have traditionally been changed at weddings.

A further step towards elder status occurs with the arrival of grandchildren. The joy that first-time grandparents show is almost too much for their neighbors at times. Yet these are the rewards of many years of life-giving. A grandfather is the most common expression of elder status. Grandfathers take interest in all their children's children. Most children love to visit their grandparents. They find there a source of love that is certainly less prone to anger and more leisurely about time than their parents who are busy. Grandparents can take the time to appreciate a child's uniqueness and special gifts.

The biological family is not the only inheritance of the elder. Their second inheritance comes in the form of a spiritual family. A spiritual family produces additional children to those who are not barren spiritually. A spiritual father is ready to form paternal bonds with children that are not biologically his own. Elders adopt men so they can train them as fathers. When elder men adopt women, it is to make them daughters. Being adopted by elder women helps younger women become good mothers and wives.

An elder becomes a father to the mothers and fathers in the community of faith. Just as grandfathers become life-givers to their own biological grandchildren, an elder pours life into the grandchildren that the Lord gives him through his spiritual children, becoming a sort of spiritual grandfather. So he continues to widen his tent pegs as his family grows.

The Story of an Elder

You ask, how does an elder get started? Let me tell you how I became an elder. It happened gradually, starting about the time my sons had both become men. Having two men for sons made me realize once more that being a man is a good thing. Being a father touched all areas of my life because it brought out the very best in me.

As a pastor and a counselor, I felt a father's grief over the ruined lives I saw. People who had started out as beautiful babies had been ravaged by abuse and neglect. I began to recognize that I was becoming an elder, a limited sort of father to those who needed one. In my relationships with others, I discovered what it means to be a supplemental father.

Strange as it may seem, other counselors, friends, and people at church began to look to me as a father figure. Often it would happen quite innocently. One friend bought a new car—his first new car. He even picked out the stereo system he wanted installed. I was excited for him and asked him to take me for a ride. What a blast we had together! Later he told me that he had always wanted his father to take an interest in his life like I had. He felt that, in a way, he had received that gift from me. What a simple gift to give!

Being a supplemental dad was not the end of the story. Some people needed more, like Renee, a wonderful young woman whom I have known for a number of years. Her father died some years ago. She has often talked to me about jobs, boyfriends, and other things people like to talk over with someone older. One day she brought this nice young man to meet me, and before you know it she was asking me to give the father's blessing at her wedding. I had become a stand-in father in her life. What a joy to watch her walk down the chapel aisle!

Rick was the first of my spiritual children to arrive as a father himself. With him, I experienced the elder's role in helping men become fathers. He needed help in almost every area of being a father.

Being an elder was immensely satisfying to me, but it took a real push from God to get me over my resistance to becoming a replacement father. Yet a replacement father was just what Eileen needed. I shopped everywhere to find her one, not because I wouldn't want to be a replacement dad, but because I felt myself unsuited for the job. I had had no experience raising daughters; I had raised sons.

As I resisted, changes took place. Over the span of several years I was given eyes to see Eileen as she really was inside, and then watched as she slowly became what I had seen. A fatherly love for her as a daughter grew so that one day I was ready to hear God's voice say, "Eileen is your daughter."

"But, Lord," I replied, "fathers are life-givers to their children, and I have not given her life."

"You have given her life," came the answer. With it I remembered Eileen's words, "I wouldn't be alive today except for you," words I had never wanted to take seriously.

So you see I'm now a proud dad—again.

But how does an elder develop a relationship that makes a difference in the lives of those with father hunger?

12.   THE ELDER: HIS SONS AND DAUGHTERS

The men's movement has drawn much of its strength from allowing men to admit they need both their fathers and each other. They have adopted the term "mentor" to mean an elder who takes a fatherly interest in a younger man.

Elders can become supplemental, stand-in, or replacement fathers to others as the need demands. Such mentor arrangements have led to lifelong commitments. Scripture mentions quite a few relationships of this sort. One of Jesus' last acts on the cross was to perform an adoption ceremony between his mother and her new adult son, John. John became a replacement son for Mary before her first son died. Thus Jesus highlighted the themes of adoption in a prominent way for his followers.

The apostle Paul develops a theology of spiritual adoption in Romans 8:15, 23; 9:24; Galatians 4:5; and Ephesians 1:5. In these passages he highlights the believers' new relationship with God. Even if they were once sinners or even non-Jews, they are now adopted children of God. Still, it is his personal practice of adopting other men that illustrates his belief in the family of God most clearly.

One example of adoption can be found in the letter Paul wrote on behalf of Onesimus, whom he called "my son ... who became my son while I was in chains" (Philem 10). It is interesting to note that in dealing with Philemon, the Christian who owned the slave Onesimus, Paul addresses him at three levels of development. Since Philemon is not a boy, Paul begins at the level of a man—perhaps Philemon wished to drive a fair and hard bargain. Paul tells him that if Onesimus owes him anything he, Paul, will pay what is due. In the interest of fairness, Paul further points out that Philemon owes his life to Paul since Paul led him to be adopted as an heir to God's kingdom.

Moving on to the level of a father, Paul encourages Philemon to give without receiving in return. Paul points out that Philemon and Onesimus are now in the same eternal family. Then, with a mention of his upcoming visit to Philemon's house, Paul gives him a nudge towards being hospitable and generous and assuming the role of an elder. In this open way, Paul is willing to meet Philemon at whatever level of development he may have reached.

Paul clearly was pleased to have a son, and Onesimus was not his only son. In writing to Titus, Paul greets him as "Titus, my true son in our common faith" (Tit 1:4). In the same way he calls Timothy "my true son in the faith" (1 Tim 1:2) and his "dear son" (2 Tim 1:2).

Paul is not alone in this practice. His dear brother, the apostle Peter, refers to Mark as his son in 1 Peter 5:13. They traveled together and Mark interpreted for the old fisherman. Mark probably wrote his Gospel as a traveling companion and catechist for Peter—at least such was the tradition in the early church. In the same way, Paul said of Timothy "as a son with his father he has served with me in the work of the gospel" (Phil 2:22). Adoption and mentoring are intricately combined in these biblical models.

The Practice of Elders Continues

Christian men continue to put in practice these basic relationships between elders and younger men. George is a divorced contractor in his late fifties. George works hard and plays hard and tries to live a life of integrity. Ten years ago George took in two men in their twenties whose lives were a mess. They had neither the skills nor the energy to manage their lives successfully. Living and working with George helped one get off drugs. Both have learned trades, skills, as well as money and time management. They have learned to live with other people and to work as well as play. George has become the father that neither had.

Mr. Hansen was a tough old Norwegian. He lived in the north woods, cut his own firewood, built his own buildings, made his own roads, and probably even cut his own hair. Mr. Hansen could pastor a church, teach a class, and sing a song with a conviction that was gripping. When he took young men under his care, they started out splitting wood or grading a road with a rake. They drank strong coffee, ate robust foods, and prayed to God as though he were right there in the woods with them.

Gruff, direct, a man of few words, Mr. Hansen thought of each boy as his responsibility. He was responsible for each boy becoming a man. He was responsible for each man becoming a father. He was responsible for each father becoming an elder. And he thought nothing of it. To Mr. Hansen these were the responsibilities of every elder, and he was not the least bit unique. His temper flared if boys did not work hard and learn their lessons, so he chose those who worked and discarded those that wouldn't. It was his way—the way of the north-woods elder.

I am glad I knew Mr. Hansen. His driveway was long and full of holes each spring. His woodpile needed careful stacking. I found the work itself no worse than my previous job in the granite quarries of North Carolina, but Mr. Hansen's quietly fierce way of grasping life and his pungent view of people were well worth the discipline I learned there—at seventeen.

Walter Watts was the pastor in Lake George. I might never have known Walt except that he had a darkroom in his basement. Thanks to my father introducing me to the community, I was offered a chance to use Walt's darkroom. Although I entered the darkroom as Earl's son, I emerged as Jim.

Walt taught me how to use his equipment and then said, "Replace the chemicals you use and you are free to use the darkroom whenever it is free." After the first few visits, I never worried about being welcome in Walt's house. Sometimes, after a long project, I would lock up the house as I quietly left Walt and his sleeping family. The skills I developed in Walt's darkroom provided me with several jobs over the years, but the trust of Walt and his family helped me become a responsible man and father. Walt was an elder who used his home, resources, and abilities to the benefit of his community.

Jim Schreiber loved people. He was probably the sort of person anyone would think of as an elder. Jim kept bees and produced his own honey. His wife Jemimah baked bread and served it too. He taught hundreds of boys to put honey on the bread first and butter second. "It keeps the honey in!" he would say. Hundreds of satisfied little boys agreed.

Jim collected tops. He had large tops, small tops, singing tops, upside-down tops. And he would do tricks with them. He spun tops on kids' heads, caught them in mid-air with their own strings, and almost never missed. Jim smiled, laughed, and talked to strangers as if he had always known them.

Jim loved to fish and take others fishing. Almost every day Jim had someone new with him in a boat full of people, teaching them to fish. His way was simple. He trolled up and down the lake with long bamboo poles for each guest until some northern pike would hit the lure. All the while he taught about the outdoors and how to enjoy the experience.

One summer Jim taught me to fish, but he did more than that. He taught me how to care for the poles, maintain an outboard motor, balance a load of passengers in a boat, watch the weather, give people a safe ride, keep the lines from getting tangled, take a fish off the hook, and help women and children feel comfortable fishing.

Jim was an elder, and I was a kid in the community. My dad and Jim worked at the same school. Because Jim cared about people, I had the best summer of my life. Jim found the people, bought gas for the boat, and I took them fishing. He gave me a place and a skill, made me feel indispensable, all because he saw something in me.

Jim helped me find a place in a world of people and the world of nature. With each new boatload, he assured us all that I had something of value to give and we were all worth getting to know.

Last night we had Denver Rice for supper. Most folks have not tried Denver Rice because they have not met Denver Brown. Denver's mother died when he was young and his wife died when he was old. My children are Denver's grandchildren; he adopted them in his eighties. He loves to see how they are doing and remembers them on holidays.

Christmas morning he stopped by with Christmas lights blinking all over his jacket to say, "Merry Christmas!" On his way he dropped off some special, high protein rice—Denver Rice. Before he left, he gave a blessing prayer and talked about the God who had brought him through the years.

Denver goes to the gym each day to exercise. He likes nutritious home-cooked meals. He filters his water and works five days a week. Denver has life to give and people to preserve and care for. Denver is an elder.

Earl is an elder in an unusual way. He is in his late seventies and loves to be informed about current events. He listens to the news on TV and radio, as well as reading magazines and newsletters. Earl reads books on current issues and keeps informed. Earl is concerned for the nation and the world. Occasionally, when he sees someone on the news whom he admires, he writes to tell the person. When he hears something that concerns him, he writes to the individual and lets him or her know. He is always careful to show how he understands their position, so that they will not take him for a crackpot. Earl's concern is international, and many people unexpectedly experience his eldership in times of need.

Earl's home is open to community groups, foreign students, and resident aliens. He is on the local school board, teaches at the senior community center, and often teaches classes at church. He is learning his fourth language and grows his own vegetables in his garden. Earl appreciates life and gives it to others. His greatest concern is that everyone know of the life that comes only from God and through Jesus come to spiritual life themselves. Earl is a life-giver. He is also my dad.

Willie is a teacher. Josie, his wife, is a teacher. They have a daughter who works part-time in a school while attending college. Willie has the stuff to be a father. When his daughter grew up, he took in a relative from his wife's side of the family named Peter who was going to school near him. Willie could see that Peter was lost and needed a dad. Even though Peter proved to be self-centered, Willie persevered. He had experienced enough losses to know the value of perseverance. There had been enough pain in his life to open his eyes. He saw that some people have to be loved just because a parent decides to love them. So it was that Willie loved Peter, talked to him, fed him, and housed him until Peter was ready to live on his own.

Dick is a younger elder. It is only in the last year that he has learned the value of adoption. Dick knows something about giving. He was always willing to help others with their children, but drew back from adopting his own spiritual children even when his natural children had gone.

Dick grew up like a mighty oak in a forest of towering redwoods. His family included mighty men of faith, missionaries to China who risked their lives for seven years just to reach one village. Dick worked in advertising rubbing shoulders with great businessmen and famous writers. Dick had a good heart. He and his wife Nancy found tires for people's cars and furniture for their homes, helped save people's homes from foreclosure, kept businesses from closing, paid for treatment expenses of orphans, helped their church reduce its debt, and brought words of encouragement and guidance to many people. In spite of all these things Dick remained a small tree in his own mind.

As more and more of the great trees around him fell to the ground, Dick began to fear that the owner of the forest would seek his life as well. And indeed it seemed that God sought his life so that Dick might become a life-giver, not just a pain preventer. Dick had one of the worst years of his life. He had one trouble after another. Everything seemed to go wrong.

"The blessing is in the adoption we receive and give," Dick would teach. "Suffering and pain are part of the process." Teaching finally had its reward, for Dick found he needed to grow to match what he taught. Dick began to adopt little scruffy trees. Proof of his growth came when another friend lost his house. Dick said quietly to me, "I could not save him even if I had the money." For Dick now knew that the life he had to give did not consist of solving people's problems but in helping boys become men, men become fathers, and fathers become elders.

A Note of Caution

The apostle Paul and others have pointed out that the hallmark of elders is their willingness to suffer for others without gaining power, control, money, or another advantage in return. Imposter elders are very sensitive to the needs of others and usually very warm in their concern, unless one crosses them or causes them any suffering. Young Americans flock to cults in great numbers seeking elders, with tragic results. A true elder is one who believes it is more blessed for him to give and you to receive than the other way around.

It is hard to exaggerate the enrichment brought to the community by true elders. Men of all ages seek the secrets known by elders that will let them see themselves, the world, and God more clearly. Elders must seek out the younger men without fear, while the younger men look to elders. In this way men will learn to be life-givers, not strangers.

How does this relate to the father hunger suffered by many women?

The Elder and His Daughters

As she got off the bus in Visalia, California, Arlis carried everything she owned in a bandanna--not much for a fourteen-year-old girl. Mark Heinz was there to meet her. Even though she did not know him well, she recognized his smile. Mark and Gloria had sent the bus ticket that had brought her here.

Arlis' mother and her eight brothers and sisters moved a great deal. She had never stayed in one place long enough to complete even one semester in school. Visalia was one more town. A shy and retiring girl, Arlis had been glad when one of her classmates invited her home on Friday night.

"Can I spend the night?" she asked her mother.

Looking around the motel room the eight of them shared, her mother answered, "All right, but be back tomorrow morning to help me clean the room."

Saturday morning Arlis rode her bicycle back to the motel, but no one answered the door. Her mother had taken everything and everyone and left town. With no other idea of what to do, Arlis went back to the home she had visited overnight where they let her stay another day.

Mark and Arlis—Father and Daughter

Sunday morning she went to church. It was a small church with only forty members. Mark was the youth minister, Gloria the director of music. Mark's dad was the pastor. With their help, Arlis contacted her grandmother in Washington state who said she could come there to live. Before she left Mark took her aside. He was saddened by the loss this young girl faced. Wishing to set her mind at rest, he told her, "If you ever need a place to stay, we will help you find one."

Arlis got a ride to Washington with an associate pastor. She was about to take the bus the rest of the way to her grandmother's house when Grandma abruptly changed her mind and told Arlis she was no longer welcome. Arlis wrote to Mark.

"We knew it would impact our daughter Carol the most," Mark remembers, "so we asked her if she wanted an older sister. Carol had been an only child for eleven years, and we left the decision up to her." Suggesting that she pray about it for awhile, her parents waited two days for their answer. Carol now says that she could have given the answer at once, for she did want an older sister. Mark sent Arlis a bus ticket so that she could return to Visalia.

Sitting in their living room that night, Mark told her, "You can't be a guest here. You will be part of the family." And as they talked, Arlis' confidence rose until she said, "Could I have a piece of bread?" The Heinzes realized that the girl had not had anything to eat, and Gloria hurried to the kitchen to fix her supper.

As they sat down to pray, Arlis asked if she could pray. It was a prayer that Mark never forgot. "Lord help me learn to obey my new mother and father," Arlis asked and with that request became a daughter to the only father she would ever know.

"I made a commitment to Arlis that she would be just like the daughter born to me," Mark remembers. "It was instantaneous. The two girls became sisters and we were a family."

Arlis got her own room painted bright yellow, even though Gloria hated yellow. Arlis loved yellow. It was her room to do with as she wanted, and she kept her door tightly closed.

A few weeks later, Gloria who was a bug about sleeping with fresh air, tiptoed into the girl's room to open a window. Arlis sat up screaming, clutching her blankets in terror. Mark and Gloria tried to comfort her to no avail. Hours later, the girl sobbed out, "If I tell you, then you won't like me anymore."

"It won't change a thing," Mark told her. Taking courage from his words, the stories poured out. It seems she had been terribly abused and lived in terror of going to sleep at night. After the stories had been told, and the tears and the sobs had subsided, Arlis rested in the arms of those who would never allow such crimes to harm her again.

The door to Arlis' room was open after that, as was the door to her heart. "She loves me so much it's almost scary," Mark tells me almost forty years later. "It is the closest to the love I have with my heavenly Father that I have ever felt. Over the years we have continued to grow closer. I am a very blessed man.

"Some people think that it must be sacrifice. We didn't have much money, but I am the one who was enriched. I only wish the church and my relatives could have accepted what our family accepted. They continued to refer to the girls as 'Arlis and your daughter' when they were both my daughters. My brother and sister have never really accepted my girl. They still invite us over and tell me not to bring Arlis."

Mark becomes tearful when he remembers how Arlis was blamed for Gloria's death because Arlis was divorced just as Gloria was dying. Some want to believe that the stress was the cause of Gloria's decline, but Mark does not believe it.

As a result of her divorce, Arlis was booted out of her church. Because of the divorce, the pastors at the church told Carol, Arlis' adoptive sister, that she should treat Arlis as though she were dead and never speak to her again. This drove a wedge between the two women, which has never been removed. It brought contention between Carol and her father, who had always been extremely close. Arlis' children turned away from the church after seeing how their mother was treated.

"I just can't reconcile this rejection by my family and church with being Christian," Mark told me sadly.

"If I could, I would ask them what the word forgiveness means. I would tell them of the joy and blessing they are missing."

Arlis was not the only girl that Mark and Gloria took into their home before Gloria died. The other girls were looking for a stand-in father but never adopted Mark and his family the way Arlis did.